Penguin Book 2665
SYNTHETIC FUN

D0170613

Jeremy Sandford was born at Eye Manor, a stately home in the border country. His father, who formerly ran the Golden Cockerell press, now opens the house to the public. His mother makes corn-dollies. Educated at Eton, he spent his youth in musical and equestrian pursuits, and he then played first clarinet in the German contingent of the R.A.F. Band. At Oxford he produced a noted musico-poetic show called *Flagrant Flowers*, and wrote a social column in *Cherwell*. Afterwards he wrote plays for the B.B.C. and broadcast on country topics in the Midlands. His play, *Dreaming Bandsmen*, was performed at the Belgrade Theatre, Coventry, with the help of a 40-piece brass band. A local reporter said he felt he'd been 'drawn through a manhole and dragged through a sewer backwards'. He married Nell Dunn, and lived with her in a Battersea slum. They have two boys. His report in the *Observer* on Britain's homeless families – among the first in the national press – provoked a storm of controversy. His documentary on the Savoy Hotel was the subject of a court injunction before finally being shown on the B.B.C., and his B.B.C. television play, *Cathy Come Home*, has been called 'a major political event'. He is currently at work on a cinema film and a book on morals. Jeremy Sandford does most of his writing on a Welsh mountain small holding where he breeds and breaks mountain ponies.

Roger Law was educated at Littleport Secondary Modern School and Cambridge School of Art, where he was Art Director of *Granta*, the University magazine. As a freelance artist he has contributed to most of the current magazines and periodicals, and he has worked for the *Observer*. He now works mainly for the *Sunday Times*. His wife Deirdre is also an illustrator, and they live with their two children in Notting Hill Gate. Roger Law is now twenty-five, and is six foot four inches tall. He and his family are planning to move to the United States.

Synthetic Fun
a short
soft
glance

by Jeremy Sandford & Roger Law

Penguin Books
Baltimore · Maryland

Penguin Books Ltd, Harmondsworth, Middlesex, England
Penguin Books Inc., 3300 Clipper Mill Road, Baltimore,
Md 21211, U.S.A.
Penguin Books Australia Ltd, Ringwood, Victoria, Australia

First published 1967
Copyright © Jeremy Sandford and Roger Law, 1967

Made and printed in Great Britain by
Hazell Watson & Viney Ltd, Aylesbury, Bucks
Set in Monotype Scotch Roman

I dedicate this book to Nell

Contents

Acknowledgements   9

Introduction   11

Fun People   19

Bloodless Bullfight   39

The Billingdon Starlight   57

Teaze   75

Seaside   101

Synthetic Fun is Needed   117

Rave   135

Synthetic Funmate   157

Notes   171

Acknowledgements

Our thanks are due to the *Observer* and the *Sunday Times* for permission to use certain of the illustrations in this book, and also for certain extracts from the text, and to Laurence Dobie, who first had the idea of sending us on an assignment together.

Synthetic fun begets blunk. Blunk was the word used by teenagers in the Madhouse Hotel at Margate to describe that state, half blocked, half drunk, induced by purple heart, other drugs, or by alcohol, or by all three together. The word is now slowly gaining acceptance generally. It is that state in which the real world can be forgotten, replaced by a dream world, synthetic euphoria. It is, perhaps, the number one ideal of our time – the goal of all of us, raddled from our daily doses of Housewives' Choice, quiz, pop music, or parlour game. We prefer to forget. Synthetic fun will help us.

Synthetic fun is the heart-shaped tablets that send you high.

Synthetic fun is the smile on the face of the Holiday Camp 'fun people' this Friday as every Friday, as they're ritually thrown into the blue blue swimming-pool.

Synthetic fun is the smile on the face of the matadors, at the Bloodless Bullfights in Spain, put on specially for the British.

Synthetic fun is the golden mile of Blackpool's Illuminations with their giant six-foot-high illuminated dwarfs and toadstools.

Synthetic fun is the ever-present constant de-sexing – freezing – pre-packing of experience, so that it may be daisy-fresh, oven ready, cellulose wrapped, and handsomely endowed with capsule prizes. Synthetic fun is that candid look on the face of the nudie languorous pin-up, inviting us into her private world with parted lips, gazing into my eyes, offering fulfilment infinite.

Synthetic fun is Soho's new post Street Offence Act gimmick of kink, titillation, teaze, clip-joints, strip-clubs.

Synthetic fun is a million pills swallowed every day, three quarter million pep pills, two and a half million sleeping pills, with which we drown or titillate our raddled senses.

Synthetic fun is the adman's dream-world in which he who reads may become once more potent, strong.

Synthetic fun is the handshake of the showman peers as they emerge from among their bison, nudists, autos, pasteboard, to autograph yet one more lavishly illustrated souvenir.

A room is decked out as Dracula's parlour, with skeletons and bowls of blood. Transmitters emit eerie shrieks. It is a publicity party for a horror film. A précis of part of the plot: ' In his hand a man holds a box. He places the box on a bench. He opens the drawer of the bench and takes from it a chisel, a small hammer, and a surgeon's knife. He opens the lid of the box. He puts on a pair of rubber gloves. He slowly lifts out the contents of the box. It is a *woman's severed head . . .* he places the head on the bench, face upwards. He picks up his knife and makes a deep, clean incision starting from the crown of the head and carrying it almost as far as the bridge of the nose. He picks up the chisel and small hammer and pressing hard on the skull with the chisel he starts tapping steadily with the hammer . . . The head splits open and the grey mass of brains spills over on the bench . . .'

Synthetic fun is those evening Telly programmes, hotted up from the morning before.

Synthetic fun is the salesman bulging free gifts for the lucky housewife.

'Give us a light,' says Barbara Snock as she relaxes in the girlie-film studios : 'I used to work in one of those big girlie shows. You know, we had to do a lot of kicks and that, but in my opinion it wasn't expressive.'

Barbara Snock is naked, as are the other girls standing around.

'I wish I wasn't so cold,' says the girl.

'As I say, we did a lot of kicks and that, but I think that's not what the fellas wanted. At a girlie show a fella wants to see girlie. *All* girlie.'

12

Synthetic fun is the disc-jockey's joke as he mouths from his heaving nest in the ocean.

Synthetic fun is the waiter's joke as he greets you to your favourite suite in the Grand Hotel Splendide Imperial Babylon.

Synthetic fun is the glossy array of fictional characters thrown up by our gossip columnists.

Synthetic fun is the smile on the face of the model girl.

Synthetic fun is the smile on the face of the whore.

Synthetic fun is the teenagers shaking, crazy, as if they'd never be old.

'This ice-cream is no good,' says the photographer as he slaves to complete his picture of the ice-cream. 'The ice-cream doesn't look like ice-cream. It's not got that *feeling*. We'll have to use mashed potatoes. Now, bite into these mashed potatoes as if you loved them. Go on. *Bite!*'

Says the photographer: 'It is the image that must be shown, thus reaching the truth. For instance custard should be represented in ads by paint. Ice should be reproduced in transparent plastic. If suds refuse to wash away with sufficient speed from a washing-machine, then blow them up the spout and then run the film backwards. Ragged meat should be trimmed at the edges with a razor blade. The drooping breasts of a girl may be pinned up with sellotape. Margarine films better than butter, egg white should be added to bowls of soup to make the bubbles last longer. However, we do have standards. For instance, sheets of glass may not be used to give the impression of polish.'

Synthetic fun is charm schools that teach 'what is and what is not acceptable in the realms of laughter.'

Synthetic fun is 'a nation that, in large degree, when the day's work is done goes home to Television.'

Synthetic fun is the sausage-eating competition, organized by the sausage makers.

Synthetic fun is the beer barrel rolling contest, organized by the beer makers.

A group of glamorous showgirls are picketing a cinema showing *Around the World With Nothing On*. Their placards say: 'Down with Nudism' and 'Up with Decollete!' The manager rushes out and grapples with the lovelies. Just another non-event dreamed up by a P.R. man.

Synthetic fun is those innumerable things that never happened, the epoch-making, shattering boredom of a whole host of non-events, the bra strap slipping from the tender shoulder of the little star.

Synthetic fun is Bunny 29 as she lollops up to you with ears and cotton-tail flapping and, like the textbook says she should, she establishes friendship with 'good eye contact', saying 'Here is your Bunny, Dolly.'

In the falsie factory, girls are putting the finishing touches to mountain after mountain of bras, shoving in foam rubber. These will go to make Venetian Blossom-Shapes, with built-up cups to give you the voluptuous bustline you have always admired. They will gleam from the windows of department stores, like beacons for the shipwrecked.

Synthetic fun is the young girl driving out with the not so young man. How happy she looks. She's hired for the night from an agency. The smile on her face has been paid for.

Synthetic fun is bikinis in turquoise cotton trimmed with white broderie anglaise, or in sky-blue towelling with matching beach shift, or candy-striped cotton, or halenca, or flame-coloured stretch nylon. These bikinis are suitable for girls from four to ten.

The new cocktail cabinet slides open its door smoothly. As it does so a concealed tape inside it asks 'What's yours, baby?'

Synthetic fun is a vast room in whose centre a computer is singing to itself, making use of its tape signal device. The programmer has made a rather unusual choice. As it stands there it is singing: 'The more We Are Together, the Merrier We'll Be.'

Synthetic fun is the ritual sitting in a traffic jam for hour after hour somewhere in Somerset on a road whose name is a number.

Synthetic fun is shampooing 'new breathless colour excitement' into your hair.

Is there an off-the-cuff definition of synthetic fun? There is.

It is fun to which, unlike conventional fun, you don't have to give very much of yourself. Pre-canned, pre-cubed, pre-heated, pre-gutted, pre-hygienized, emasculated, dialled-for instant entertainment.

People make money from it. The desire to make money — not love — is the reason for its existence.

Say what is the social need for synthetic fun? The answer comes: Affluence – leisure – and above all – boredom – terrifying, hitherto unprecedented, BOREDOM.

Bertrand Russell says: 'At least half the sins of mankind are caused by attempts to escape boredom.'

The crime rate in Britain is at its highest in the afternoon on Sunday – that time of maximum leisure, when we should be most happy.

Kingsley Amis says: 'Boredom of a range and power we can barely conceive is my personal tip for the chief enemy of the psyche in time to come.'

Boredom has thrown up, like an ugly pustule, in blunk, its own malaise. And, witnessing the world of synthetic fun, we may be struck by the amazing absence in Britain of any real thinking about leisure, any real orientation of education towards leisure, any real attempt at planning for it.

Synthetic fun, cellulose-wrapped, through-putting, handsomely with-it!

Fresh as a fish in a deepfreeze, pre-packed, cubed, just hot it up and tip onto a cold plate!

Hygienic, containing no vitamins at all!

Meanwhile, back at the Madhouse Hotel . . .

There are teenagers camped on the floor on old bits of newspaper, on sleeping-bags, some high on pot, some high on the raddled music of radios, some drunk. All high on something, most blunk.

One of those lying in a typical blunk stupor is not like the rest.

He has a gangrenous leg, producing quite a stench, and he's passing the time in groaning. Confused words emerge: 'Help', 'Doctor'. Sometimes his groaning gets strident. It is intruding on the others' dreams. That's when they, each blunk in his own particular manner, get bugged. 'Aw shit! Shite! Shut up! Cool man!' In another but similar place he died later, and I, when I saw him lying there realized then that:

Synthetic fun is needed.

Fun People

Campers swimming beneath the sodden flags of all nations in the blue blue swimming-bath, beneath polyvynil parrots and plastic vine leaves.

Campers in The Tudor Ballroom being instructed in ballroom dancing in their shirt sleeves.

Campers being given Holy Mass in the Sports Pavilion.

Campers being put through an Inter-House Quiz in the Twist'n'Shout Ballroom.

Campers filling in their cards in the Bingo Stadium.

Campers being put through the Knobbly Knees competition in the Hawaiian Ballroom.

Young campers screaming their heads off in the pastel décor of the communal nurseries.

Teenage campers chasing each other lyrically and endlessly round the balconies and chalets.

Campers aboard a comic train, which takes them through a hardboard Gothic arch, chugs on past the car park, past concrete dragons and papier maché armadillos.

Campers queueing for their turn to eat in the vast dining-room.

Campers sleeping, like forgotten rubbish, in the corners of the lounges and quiet rooms . . .

Campers boating on a long black pond, surrounded by tall iron and barbed-wire fences.

A young camper being sick into the swimming-bath. She says: 'It was drinking that chalet water what did it.'

Campers twisting in the Twist'n'Shout Ballroom, their hand-bags laid out neatly on the floor beside them.

Campers sitting on balconies in their curlers.

Campers in vast theatres, watching variety shows.

Campers peering at photos in the camp photographic shop, with its notice 'Memories are Precious. Stimulate them with Photos.'

Campers on the sun terrace, looking out through plate glass to where the grey waters swim in, edged with golden foam.

And by night, nurses speed through the camp on bicycles, listening for the sound of crying ...

The ironmesh gates swing open, and the security guards step back, and the buses and taxis surge in, past the indoor and outdoor swimming baths, along the black concrete, nosing through the crowds of campers, past the vast hangar containing the Tropicana Bar, Hairdressing Salons, TV Lounge, and Ballrooms, nose in amongst the campers already swarming the streets in their hundreds. From the windows of their bus two Scottish boys cheer wildly at a couple of girls in bikinis and Hawaiian hats inscribed 'Kiss me Quick', eating ices. First sight of young female flesh ... and the 'Fun People' are here too in their gay gold and scarlet uniforms, ready with a quip, shouting: 'Oh, for goodness sake don't come here!' but undeterred the campers climb down from their buses and enter the Reception Building.

There are many hundreds of people in this camp coming in today and many hundreds leaving. To wander among its chalets is often to be lost in a maze of doors and terraces, windows, roses, which stretch out of sight. Great buildings rise up, huge hulks, at the end of these vistas; theatres, dance halls, indoor swimming baths, reception buildings, dining halls. Notices which stand up against the sky proclaim: 'TWIST, SHAKE, AND CHA CHA BALLROOM' and 'ROSE BUILDINGS'.

The camp radio is playing as the campers arrive, through powerful loudspeakers hidden behind rose bushes. Rain falls in a light drizzle across the sports field. Now two of the Fun People are wrestling, trying to throw each other into the blue blue pool.

The perimeter fence and the vast gates are tall, in-turned, sprouting barbed wire. There are only two gates and from now on campers must show their chalet keys before they're let in or out. But there will be little desire to escape.

The camp is like a military camp in which the swimming-bath has replaced the parade-ground. In the reception halls to which the new arrivals now make their way, illuminated pink and white plastic globes hang from the ceiling, alternating with baskets containing plastic flowers. The campers drift in, mortals in the antechamber to heaven; this is what we've been dreaming of, through the winter. Here comes a plump old grannie in a black dress with sequins on it, and an imitation diamond necklace ... a little girl in a white 'fairy' dress, looking like an angel, carrying a small black piccaninny doll ... a farm labourer, looking embarrassed in his suit and striped shirt ... girls with tall sticky beehive hair styles, and golden sandals and belts ... young men in black leather jackets and tight blue jeans ...

On the walls pictures of the 'great old man', the proprietor, presiding at various events, awarding prizes for the 'Knobbly Knees' contest and for the 'Holiday Princess'.

There's luggage everywhere. Overawed budgies cluster in a gilded cage. A voice from a loudspeaker concealed behind plastic roses announces: 'Campers, while you are waiting you may sit in the Ugly Duckling coffee bar, adjacent to this Reception.' Campers queue up for their chalet keys and meal tickets.

They shuffle on into the camp.

The roses here: some lines of chalets almost submerged beneath them: chalets whose two hanging storeys of sagging wood are painted with bizarre letters of identification: PCT 12 or VBW 14. Cars quietly stew in their hundreds in an enclosure outside, forgotten. Campers gossip at the chalet doorways, hanging out their washing. Between some of the two-storey lines of chalets trees as well as roses grow so high that their branches glut windows and trail across the hanging terraces where boys stand, their chests braced, ready to be photographed. Or girls stand on the sagging balconies leaning over, waiting.

A group of young men, their hair permed and falling in luxurious 'Oscar Wilde' curlicues and bangs down to their shoulders stroll back and forth from xz 4 to xz 142 – the teenage block. They wear black jeans and T-shirts that say 'Moscow University'. Seeing a girl they fancy they shout in chorus: 'There's Joan There's Joan There's Joan.'

Over their heads the loudspeaker emits an advertisement for beer, followed by one for the camp they're in. Then it yells: 'Go and buy an ice-cream, go and buy an ice-cream, go and buy an ice-cream quick.'

Jackie Thomas of Wentworth: 'This place is the best. We went to Jersey last year and we got nothing. People go there, you know, for the weather. Whereas here, it's known what they come for, it's known. After the first few nights you'll see most of the birds have love-bites on their necks, we call it chalet-rash. The fellas come for the birds and the birds come for the fellas.'

Bingo goes on non-stop. Like in a cathedral where worship never ceases, there's always some part of the Camp in which Bingo is in session. The last session of all is at eleven at night and continues, even after 'Good night Campers', into the early hours of the morning.

Alan Moore, steelworker from Sheffield: 'It's the landladies that send the people here. Last year we went to Wales. Terrible it was. We were at 'Berkeley'. The sort of place, the moment you step in at the door, you can feel your morale sinking. The first room I saw I said I wouldn't have it. Didn't I? Threw down my baggage on the ground. And the waitress never changed her dress, and we had nothing to eat, we were hungry after every meal, and nowhere to go in the evening except sit on the hard chairs in the dining-room, not even the Telly, and nowhere to put the children; this place is better. That was ten a week, for nothing, whereas this is fifteen, all found.'

Three beats pass – black glasses, black flowing shoulder-length hair, jeans jackets and jeans.

Dyllis Framley, farm labourer's wife from Herefordshire: 'It's the fact that the kiddies are looked after. When we got back home last time there was a letter from the camp saying they hoped we'd had a good time. My Linda said she wished we could stay for ever, but I said "You couldn't really. It's not real, you see. It doesn't belong to the real world. It's more like fairyland."'

From behind a plastic rose bush the Camp Radio strikes up. It sings:

> 'Hello campers
> There's a good time on the way
> For wet or fine, the sun will always shine
> On your goodtime holiday.'

Cheerfulness is in the control of the fun people, handsome young men and girls who wear fabulous scarlet and gold uniforms, nicknamed 'the Goldjackets'. They hover round the glum campers like prefects at a school speech day or young officers at a pass-out parade. If you come by train these fun-loving people are there at the station to meet you, shouting: 'Don't come here! Go back home! It's horrible!' They get £9 a week and are proud of their jobs, and they form the aristocracy of the camp. On Thursdays they're ritually thrown into the pool. They come usually from the fringe of showbiz and in the evenings put on the shows in the camp theatres. They have special chalets which, unlike the campers' chalets, have gas rings; they keep charts showing their success with the campers. In the winter they work in pantomime, go on the dole, work in the winter sales in London's big stores, or otherwise relapse into obscurity.

Two Goldjackets teasing a girl Goldjacket: 'I'll tell the old man about you, your brass buttons aren't polished.'

'Anyway, stand up when you speak to the sergeant.'

'And you've only got forty-three pleats in your skirt, I'll tell the boss about you.'

'Don't you tell anyone. She's got a secret. She's only been a Goldjacket for a day.'

The walls have pictures of swans floating through trellis, lined with rose-coloured paper. There are plastic flowers hanging down.

The Camp Radio: 'Here's a suggestion for your morning's entertainment – meet Uncle Len in the Venetian Lounge.'

We go. It is competition time. As we enter, a few thousand bulbs, lemon and orange, light up in the ceiling.

Uncle Len is a sporty fellow who wears a brilliant blazer with the camp emblem on it. 'Well, this morning is mainly for the children. But all are welcome. We're going to have quite a number of competitions before we're finished, in fact we've got competitions going throughout the day. To help us out we've got various Aunties. Let's see, our chief Auntie is Auntie Meg. There she is. Isn't she a nice Auntie? Her name is Auntie Meg. Then there's our junior campers' leading Auntie, her name is Auntie Cath. Yes, Auntie Cath. But I call her matchsticks.

'Now all these Aunties have their funny little habits. Auntie Jane, for instance, collects bottle tops. Auntie June collects threepenny bits. Auntie Cath collects boyfriends.

'Now that man over there with the television set, he's a photographer. Why is that little girl over there standing up?

26

What do you think, children? I think she must be like a railway engine, she's got a tender behind.

'Now what other Uncles and Aunties have we got? Ah, here there's a table-tennis coach, specially sent down from London, he's a coach, that's not the thing you go down to the sea in for excursions, no, it's a coach, a table-tennis coach.

'Then there's Uncle Tommy and his magic – and what else have we – ah, here is the camp padre, a big hand –'

The camp padre skips on to the stage, holding up his vestments: 'Good morning, junior campers. A few weeks ago I was browsing through the newspapers without a thought in my mind. Then my eye was caught by a small news item. It mentioned that the Lotus firm had perfected a new racing car. We shall be hearing more about the Lotus racing car in the current week. And more too about the word of our Lord Jesus Christ.'

He skips off. Uncle Len says: 'That's about all, I think. Oh yes, I forgot just two more. That's Auntie Mary and Auntie Val. Auntie Mary and Auntie Val are singists. Yes, they're very good singists.

'So, here we are, let's get going on the competitions. Everyone ready? All of you warmed up? Oh good. And here we've got our Walls Ice-Cream person all ready, in case any of you is a bit hot. Anyone a bit hot? Anyone hot? Auntie Mary, I think we've got all these children warmed up.'

When the children leave the Venetian Ballroom we stay behind. A few minutes later it's filled once more, this time with adults.

Uncle Len is still on duty, although he now wears a more sophisticated face. He says: 'And now to introduce you to some of your friends in the red and the gold. And to introduce you to the Goldjacket in charge of whatever block you may happen to be in. First – Exeter Block.'

The Goldjacket in charge of Exeter Block leaps up on the stage. Young for so responsible a position, he seems the typical public schoolboy, gold-haired, clean-limbed. He shouts: 'Hi folks! Now, all you lucky people in Exeter Block, I want you to do this thing for me. When you see me, shout 'Mashed Potatoes!' Well, I've been asked to say a few words about this block, well it's the best block, we all know that, the best block. I must admit it.' This statement is followed by cheers and boos.

'Now for Plymouth Block.'

The young Master of Plymouth Block sprints up on the stage: 'Well folks, Plymouth Block is the best, we all know that, it's the best, I have to admit it, the best, now whenever you see me, will you please all shout like this: 'Zigga Zagga Zigga Zagga. Ho! Ho! Ho!'

Outside, the Radio speaks forth through loudspeakers hidden among the roses: 'Campers may care to note that a cash Bingo Session is now in operation in the Bingo Hall.'

We wander on, passing a large boating lake, black in colour, surrounded by tall ironmesh fences, and campers in the Choco-Bar peering through a tropical aquarium at other campers swimming in the indoor swimming bath.

We pass the two Television rooms, tatty oblong chambers with cinema seats, hot and empty.

We pass a large hall hung with pink, white and blue drapes, and a canvas backcloth depicting an altar and a stained-glass window. Goldjackets are standing around with special pie faces and a few hundred campers are singing a hymn, backed by the camp orchestra. The hymn finishes. The padre skips on the stage. He announces: 'A few weeks ago I was browsing through the papers without a thought in my head when I came upon an item which seized my attention, that a new range of designs had been spearheaded by the mighty Lotus Motor Company . . .'

The rattle of the scenic and the thump of the juke-box comes distantly to us here.

We continue on our way, through the Twist'n'Shake Ballroom with its silver-paper hangings. Here a five-piece band is playing for campers, indulging in ballroom dancing in their shirtsleeves. A couple of middle-aged Goldjackets are there to partner the lonely.

At the farther end we reach a luxurious fitted-carpet lounge, where hydrangeas bloom in pots and swaying lace curtains give onto views of chalets stretching away out of sight. People are wandering among them now with a rash of large paper rosettes on their chests.

We arrive at the Sea Terrace, a place that looks out through glass onto the ocean foam. The grey waters with their golden crests sail in. There are large plastic umbrellas here that stand in red white and blue barrels. The ends of these staunch chalets have been dolled up to look like Spain, with pink pillars, balconies, false french windows.

'Right, hold your numbers in your right hand if you would please and smile. That's right. Remember that the smile is part of your personality. Would the next three come up please? Thank you. For those of you who have only just arrived in the audience, may I announce that we are now in the middle of our personality parade. Now, the papers have just been collected, and they're being vetted by the scrutineer, and in a moment we will no doubt know which of the young ladies we want to invite to come back. Meanwhile I don't see any reason why we shouldn't have a slow walk round the judges do you? Incidentally, following this competition we have another one for the grandads, so if you're a grandad I hope you'll compete. Right, now we have the results coming up now . . . as you are well aware, we always announce the third prize first . . .'

Other contests present a bird's-eye view of various national types or ideals; the Holiday Princess, Dad and His Lad,

Family Group, Mother and Child, Glamorous Grandmother, Grand Grandads, and Knobbly Knees.

Only occasionally does the strain of always having to be friendly tell on the Goldjackets. At the Holiday Princess competition they get to work on members of the audience to get them to compete. Sometimes they persuade a hideous girl to compete. Or choose a tiny woman, almost a dwarf, to go on the stage flanked by two tall beauties. 'Ee, stand up in the middle there!'

The Holiday Princess winners are chosen. First prize has a light blue halter top and a blue, pink and red striped bottom. Second prize has a blue one-piece with panels over the bosom decorated with cherries.

This over, the Holiday Princesses must themselves sit down to judge the 'Knobbly Knees' contest. This involves fifty men rolling their trousers above their knees and parading themselves in front of the swimsuited lovelies. Then they must do unexpected things like flaunt themselves like puffs, or line up close together and bend so that they all fall down. As they do this a man, specially provided, makes the sound of creaking knees through a microphone.

Finally, they all form a queue to give the 'lovelies' a kiss. Some of the campers may seem sheepish but all shyness is dispelled when the gay Goldjackets squeeze in for a turn when no one's looking, linger long and lovingly over the swelling swathes of the lovelies.

The Glamorous Grandmother competition follows, and anyone worried about the guts of the present-day British would have their fears put to rest by one sight of these proud British matrons, landladies to a man, one might think.

'Right ladies, hold your number cards in your right hand please, and smile, smile, remember that the smile is the expression of your personality . . . for those of you who have only just arrived in the ballroom this is to remind you that this is our personality parade for Glamorous Grandmothers ... right, the papers have just been collected from the judges ... we have the result coming up now, yes, and now we have the winner, No. 14!'

No. 14 strumps up onto the stage. She wears a pink, grey and white costume, restrained by a thin ribbon belt. 'We'd like to know your name. Your name? Mrs Potter.'

'And now we have the Grand Grandad Competition. Grandads will be marked for two things: both their personality and their general appearance.' The Grandads, chests puffed out, arms stiffly by their sides, march up in their dark suits desperately smiling.

The luxurious grey chairs are bulky, stuffed with foam rubber. The ceiling has panels in lemon and light blue. Underfoot, fitted rose-emblazoned carpets.

The camp assistant manager mouths through a mike: 'Folks, this morning with many hundreds of campers coming in and many hundreds going out I hope you'll understand that things may get a little chaotic.' Before him lounge those campers who can afford to stay a second week. 'It's a buffet luncheon today, but from then on it'll be the same as usual, *quite* a lot of the entertainment will be different although of course it won't all be. The Variety Company is presenting yet another new show for you. The Goldjackets, I'm sure you've all got to know and like the Goldjackets while you've been here, so any time you see any of us in the streets I hope you'll come up to us and say Hullo Mike or Lou, or whatever it is, Come and have a drink ... They're handing round badges for you now, I see. These are Second Week badges, you should wear them as well as your regular badges, they're to show us, just in case we don't recognize you straight off, that you're old friends. Now the coffee here this morning is all free, I hope you'll feel at liberty to drink as much as you desire. And just to pass the time till dinner now we're going to have three games of Bingo. Three games of Bingo for these valuable prizes. There's a teapot, not a pot-tee but a tea-pot, a wastepaper basket, and an umbrella. Now the Goldjackets are going to take over. As you know, things have a way of happening when the Goldjackets are around.'

A small but energetic Goldjacket: 'I must confess, you're the happiest set of Bingo fans I've ever set eyes on.' The glum rows stretch away in front of him. 'Now, can I have a little boy to turn the cage?' A little boy is provided.

' . . . all the fours, droopy drawers, five and seven, Heinzes Beenzes, legs, number eleven, legs.' Everyone whistles at this exciting mention of legs and the Goldjacket says through his mike: 'Dirty sods!'

Bye Bye

Good-bye now: the campers in suits; only their funny hats and badges to remind them, and the buses and taxis permeating to parts of the camp where they wouldn't normally go.

They wear straw hats loaded with camp badges and rosettes with the name of their house and dining halls.

They cluster round the Goldjackets to get their autographs.

A group of kids in T-shirts saying HONDA and SURF CITY and MOD GIRL kissing and putting ice-cream down each other's backs till the buses bearing the name of their home town pull in.

At one side of the blue blue swimming-bath floats a pile of sick.

A little boy and girl of about fourteen, hand in hand, briefly in love before the bus leaves . . .

People are throwing pennies into a pool filled with plastic water-lilies, where disinfected warm water flows into a plastic bowl. They do it because they hope they'll return.

Many will. Many will go on to other camps, collecting badges that they'll wear on their lapels, like medals won in war.

And we, who have seen it before, are in the massive drinking saloon of yet another camp in which, later that night, a thousand new campers will get down to drinking in earnest. The beautiful near-empty nearly dark room stretches away, dark

wood, crimson velvet and mirrors, mahogany, ceilinged with chandeliers with coloured bulbs in them, dark beams. Behind the immensely long bars stand students and others in striped shirts and leather waistcoats. One of them shouts at a pair of young girls: 'Are you down here on holiday? Oh, well you'll have to work hard then.'

Tina, one of the chalet maids, says: 'I'll tell you why this camp has such a sort of tepid atmosphere. It's because everyone is passing time. Staff and campers are the same. It's a strange thing, an extraordinary atmosphere here. You get such low wages that you could say we were all being exploited, except that people choose to come here, for them it's a way of passing the summer, they don't have to come, so you can't really say it that we're being exploited. It appeals to them who don't want to do anything with their lives, the drifters.'

Ronnie, one of the kitchen staff: 'The way I see it, you get six ten a week, and all the girls you want.'

Tina: 'It's like all catering only more so: it appeals to the drifters. People make love here compulsively. Men have three or four girls each night, in various parts of the beach. Almost everything we ever get paid goes straight back to the boss in drink. When I first came here I couldn't stop crying. But now I find I'm calling the bloody camp 'home'.

Tina was from a middle-class background in Berkhamstead. She took a typist's course, failed it. She walked out of home after a row with her Dad, ran away to be a Goldjacket. But she finished as a chalet maid.

'It's amazing the way the campers go for the staff. They want to identify themselves with the camp, I suppose. They pass through here in the happiest week of their year, they wish they could stay, and we really *do* stay. They realize that. They want to make the relationship permanent.'

Goodie: 'I saw you making the relationship permanent last night. In the Maverick Quiet Room.'

Ronnie: 'It's them limbs of yours what gets the campers.'

Linda, a petite brunette chalet maid with long hair coming down to her shoulders: 'I got a new motto today: practise promiscuity and save the chalet maid. You can take it two ways see. First, if the campers share each other's beds then there's less beds for the chalet maids to make, and second, they go after each other and leave us alone.'

Tina: 'It's not my fault. I was going with Rod Richie wasn't I? (That's the resident beat group singer.) But now he's going out with the campers en't he? Wants variety. Well, he no more got no time for me.'

Ronnie: 'By the way, there's a party in the staff hostel tonight. Sixty gallons of coarse cider up from Somerset. Come if you like. And there's forty-three women coming and all of them slags.'

The meeting place for the party is in chalet XL 6650 and fifteen people are already squashed into the little room that smells of disinfected concrete.

Ronnie is wearing dark glasses and when he takes them off his eyes are livid.

'What happened to you?'

'Oh, the Security got me.'

Most utopias ever dreamed or desired by man have had some built-in violence which takes over where kindness fails. The security guards in their peaked caps and brilliant gold uniforms do it here.

The girls' dormitories have a notice over their entrance: 'Any male found in female staff dormitories will be instantly terminated.' The security rule by fear and beat-up or instantly evict, sometimes without much reason, to keep their image in trim.

A banging on the door and the huge bulk of two gold-clad security men enter.

'Now pack it in you lot, what's this, a party? Who are you anyway? Staff, staff, staff, and you're staff . . . you're staff . . . pack it in. And don't think you're going along to the hostel. We've broken that up already.'

We go out through the sea gate, onto the yielding shingle, beside the grey hideous laced foam of a synthetic-seeming sea.

We trudge along the shore till we reach a wartime dugout, half clogged up with shingle.

Inside the door it smells of dead fish and urine.

A little paraffin lamp. A guitar quietly twanging.

It's hard to see who's there, about forty people, I think.

Tina: 'I can't describe it really. Our staff dormitories are over the ballroom where they have all the competitions. The walls are thin, and the floors. Every single hour of the day you hear these competitions droning on. You feel you're being brainwashed.'

More and more people are piling into the bunker now, and the oil lamp in the middle of the floor is flickering.

The twang of fairly incompetent folk music.

The lamp goes out. Tina's brother says: 'I'll put some more in.'

He picks up the paraffin container, opens the side of the lamp, and pours it in. Then there's a sheet of flame and a roar like a boiler igniting. Everyone recoils, some bashing their skulls against the ceiling. The boy is on fire. They bundle him out to the sea, immerse him. But it is too late. When he returns, dripping, his face, in the flickering glow of the lamp, is the face of a monster.

(*The sketches of holiday camps in this section were a composite picture, based on three different places, each run by a different proprietor.*)

BLOODLESS BULLFIGHT

Package-trip British tourists queue in the sweltering sunlight, bewildered on the hot runway of some foreign airport.

Package-trip British tourists take snapshots of each other, drinking at rickety caf tables, being rooked by ever-smiling waiters.

Package-trip British tourists stand deliberating in souvenir shops, whether to buy a bullfight poster with their name added beneath that of Ordoñez, or a mahogany back-scratcher.

Package-trip British tourists hang around waiting to complain to their Resident Hostess about the disgusting menus.

Package-trip British tourists bask in the hot blowing sand of the shore. They are half submerged and hate the Germans.

Package-trip British tourists see nothing strange in the fact that hundreds and hundreds of miles of the Mediterranean seaboard have been built up in the image of their dreams . . .

The Day I discovered that Beaches Mean Fun – The Fiascotour Way

As she lounges on the hotel terrace beneath striped umbrellas, the bikini-clad lass is reading a brochure whose cover shows a bikini-clad lass lounging on a hotel terrace beneath striped umbrellas. She's writing:

Dear Pam,
One day I decided it was high time I left boring old England and took my hols in the Med. But I really never thought I'd be able to manage it until I got to hear about the *Fiascotour* way.

The first thing that I noticed about my *Fiascotour* Holiday was it was all so incredibly easy. At Gatwick Airstrip, for instance, I was met by a delightful *Fiasco* courier.

Then – fun on the plane. Imagine my amazement to find myself having a delicious snack high over the Channel. At the romantic Airport the plane was met by a bus. I felt like a filmstar. I knew this would be a holiday to remember.

The *Fiascotel* was top-notch. Excitingly designed by top *Fiasco* designers – ultra-modern decor, subdued but striking colour-scheme – I had to have a quick look at my booking-form to make sure I hadn't strayed into a millionaire's paradise.

During the long long sunny days I just strolled into the sea and swam around until I cooled off a bit.

The twilight evenings were paradise. A walk under the starlit sky, a midnight swim, *fun* at a wine tasting party, a *chat* with a *new* friend . . . I also went on some *exciting Fiasco excursions* . . . and a few on my own . . .

Pretentious, without distinction, but with their own air of phoney romance the hotels rise floor after floor, balcony after concrete balcony, to vast heights, and at the summit of these cliff-like edifices stand up their names, exotic in ten-feet-high pink or purple neon: *Regina Christina, Oceana, Balmoral, Tropicana, Mediterraneo, Gran Palacia*. In between there are areas of sandy marsh, not yet built over, with notices claiming 'Se Vende' amid the rubbish.

Across the terraces and patios comes at most times of day a certain type of amplified music, blending with the chirp of crickets, most often the moaning voluptuous wordless chant of a woman, seemingly utterly abandoned, singing heartwhole from the depths of an inexpressible erotic candour. In front of the terraces a strip of black tarmac is laid across the sand, down which buses and taxis hurtle. Then there is the beach: a beach thick with bodies, on the ground, on deck chairs, beneath straw umbrellas, British bodies, bodies that lie like petrified creatures, as if excavated from some long since lava-encased city. There are little shanties made from driftwood and pine branches. They have hand-painted names, '*Helados La Sirena*', '*Balmoral*'. The British stagger to them for refreshment, then return to swelter. Sometimes the bodies are veiled in a thin layer of drifting sand. Sometimes the flesh has gone raw, the top layer of skin being ruthlessly stripped from the carcase. Some have sticking plaster or bandages adhering to afflicted parts such as nose or shoulder.

A foreman at a Swindon factory, his brilliant purplish chest emerging from swimming-trunks with a salmon motif, lying semi-submerged in scalding driving sand: 'It stones you. The first two days your British fellow comes out here it really knocks him for six, he creeps about, you know, don't know what hit him. And then, suddenly, it's like a great weight being lifted off you that's been pushing you down all your days. It's the sun that gives freedom. You know what a problem footwear is back home. Well, here no one minds. They really do not mind what you wear on your feet. Look what I'm wearing now! Just look at us! Just look what we're wearing! Look at my wife! Take a look at me!' He pauses a moment stunned, then continues: 'You don't care here, nobody is quizzing you all the time in the street, you can drink if you want, go out, get drunk, come back not worried a damn!'

His wife, apple-faced, wearing a white jumper over a green and beige one-piece swimsuit: 'They have no sense of time here. George finds that, having rather a regular type of time schedule as regards his life in Britain, it's a great relief not to need to know what the time is. Here there are no clocks! No, you never see a clock. They don't care about them! I wanted to buy one for a present. I couldn't find one!'

'I think the food is rather disgusting though.'

'I don't. I find it all right. Only, there's too much of it.'

From the hotel patio a lyrical amplified woman's voice mouths 'I've got you ... I'm crazy about you, I'm absolutely the ...'

'I think the bullfights are disgusting.'

'It's not what they do, it's the way they do it.'

'Well I say it's only a sport, enit?'

'The principal reason for Continental travel is, it's a status symbol. The people next door do it, so you do it too.'

'What did it finally was a terrible holiday in Wales . . .'

Mr Alan Davies, Ebbw Vale steelworker, a can of tepid beer half raised to his lips: 'I think that boozing is the most important of all, in my opinion. Being able to booze through the day, it gears the whole day, doesn't it, it ticks, slip in for a drink . . . any time . . .'

Mrs Iris Stoggett, Berkshire mother of a young electricity showman: 'I'm taking quite a number of presents home for them as didn't come, as I think is only fair. I got bullfight posters for my two nephews, with their names written in just like real bullfighters. I got a flamenco dancer with a bulb inside that lights up. I got fans with pictures of the Spanish mountains, and two old Toledo swords very reasonable.'

Romance

'They smell of garlic. Otherwise they're all right. Only, when you've been dancing with them, they won't let you go. It's rather pathetic. But their own girls are all kept locked up. Anyway, they're no different to pathetic little men everywhere.'

A trainee hotel receptionist from Huddersfield: 'They follow after you at night, shouting after you in every language they can think of, 'What's your name! You're beautiful!'

A Welsh schoolmistress: 'Often I'm afraid, even during the daylight hours in the older streets I've received what I can only describe as a backhander.'

Mary Dodgson, a young Nannie out on her employers' annual holiday: 'I thought he was nice, so when he asked me out, I was pleased. I put on a flared fitted dress I'd brought out for

43

just such an occasion, it's got flares round the top and bottom and it's quite revealing, at the top I mean. Never again. I'm going to stick to British boys in future. I kept on trying to strike up a conversation with him. But all he seemed to want to do was to snog – in public! When we got back it was worse. He got very nasty. He seemed to be only after One Thing.'

In *Alfies London Bar* overlooking the esplanade, the Spanish bartender: 'I have slippt with much British girl, young, kind, obedient. Every night to the wood. Girls coming here expecting every Spaniard a Casanova, expect him experiment and he do.' He demonstrates, batting his eyes: 'Hullo, may I embrace your hand? Let me take off your glasses, so I can gaze into your beautiful eyes.' He snatches the glasses from nearby girls. 'They are not used to such trifles from British men. Then I go with Scottish girl. I think to marry her. She is young, kind, obedient. We have custom Spanish mentality if girl is broken we throw her out. Different peoples learn different things at mother's knee, this is what we learns. So when I see she is slippt I throw her out.'

In a beautiful seventeenth-century palazzo in one of the twisting back streets there's a courtyard, and the rooms have patchy wall paintings on the walls and chandeliers hanging from the ceiling. Furnished with smart Naafi-type tables in red and white plastic, it provides one of the cheaper package holidays. On a half-broken chair the balding proprietor sits putting records of flamenco on a record player.

An attractive girl, shortly to marry into the catering business in Cornwall: 'I had suspected it might be something like this, but I never thought it could be so wonderful. When we arrived, in the middle of the night, I couldn't believe how lucky I'd been. We went into the courtyard, it was so antique and romantic, then into the rooms with their wall paintings and their chandeliers – it was wonderful! I sank into bed, and the following morning, I can't describe it, waking up and looking up at the bedroom ceiling, all cherubs and flowers peeling off, and the narrow little street, I saw it was called, of all things, the Calle Ecce Homo! And nearby somewhere there was a cock crowing, and someone was singing some fantastic old Moorish melody. Next year I'm going to have to be working in the summer time, but I'll always remember this.'

At the other end of the noble apartment, buying Eno's by the glass and then chasing it with Coca-cola, sit four North Country boys and they don't share her enthusiasm.

Bob Pratt of Stogg Lane, Huddersfield: 'I think this place is disgusting. When we first saw it we wanted to ask for our money back. The food too, it's disgusting. And our rooms are over the kitchens, so you smell it even when you're not eating it. To get to any beach at all, well, it's about half an hour lurching along in the filthiest bus you ever saw ... The thing is, the brochure gave no indication that we were such a long way from the sea.'

NOTICE

Big fluency of people at seaside, swimming pools, lakes, ponds, and rivers in summertime owing to tourism reasons claim for a revision of regulations about morality and good customs so that same will be fulfilled for benefit of principles they represent and of the civic spirit that must prevail in public places ...

A The use of bathing suit along streets of town is most strongly forbidden.

B The use of shorts in cities center also is most strongly forbidden.

A bar hung with bulls' heads, clippings from 'Private Eye'. Gordon Whitehead, a man with a red face, shock of white hair standing straight up from it, sways as he says: 'The point is, there's a credit and debit to life. And here, for me, the credit

45

is greater than the debit. Sunlight – sea – cheap drink – all seems to suit my wandering way of life. Came here from Iceland as it happens. Been here seven years. Got a factory here brews beer as good as the British, we say. Got em working three shifts, round the clock. Good workers. Dashed good provided you make em. This is the worst time of year for this island. Get all the scum of Europe.'

Laura, attractive, ex-showbiz: 'I came here on holiday seven years ago. Got offered a job looking after a bar. So I stayed. I wouldn't like to live here if I wasn't working though. Too easy to go on the bottle.'

James Rothsay-Clarke, a retired colonel: 'Your Briton is by no means the most unpopular specimen on the island. The Scandinavians are worse. You know, their pubs close at six in the evenings so their first aim when they get here is to get sozzled. You can see them standing at the bar here, scarcely able to shovel another drink down their gullets. Then they stagger out at closing time, two in the morning, totally drunk, and very often nasty with it.'

James Huntingdon Stafford, an aristocratic shambling person, once a well-known bullfighter: 'I've been noticing things recently. I've been helping out a friend behind the bar, and to do that you've got to watch. I've taken to observing and I've observed the most 'straordinary things. That first night there was a businessman and his secretary here, a woman, whose husband had gone back to England, trying to make it with a friend of mine over here, two queens over there, I stood back reeling. I mean I suppose these things go on all the time, but by God I'd never noticed them before I had to work in a menial role for my living.'

Jonathan Egerton, salesman from Manchester: 'When we first went to my room, for instance, there was a terrible stink. One of the drains had burst actually, I went to the Reception or whatever they call it to tell her, it was all 'No comprendo, no comprendo,' you know, so then I took her by the arm and led her into my room, then I staggered about a bit, I screamed, and held my nose. She understood all right.'

Janice Growcott, soft drinks salesgirl from Manchester, her plump face and dark piled-up hair, her plump roasted breasts swelling out her halter-neck bikini: ' Well, in the morning we're always down late for breakfast!!! Then we go down for a dip, sometimes don't, just lounge around in the sun. Then after lunch we have a siesta, go out to the beach again, perhaps a little bit of shopping, then supper – and then after that we go dancing, in one of those open-air places.'

Marylyn Turpin, Welsh schoolteacher from Port Talbot with ruby lips and a plump agreeable face and her hair cut in page-boy style, her white skin occasionally bursting out into purple patches where the sun has got her: 'Last year we went on what they called an "Away From It All" holiday. It *was* away from it all! Half-way up a mountain! It was a lovely hotel like they said, but what they didn't say was, it was ten thousand feet up in the sky, up on the side of the mountain, on the edge of a precipice; there wasn't another house for miles, plenty others you could see, but they were down in the valley, ten thousand feet below . . . people too, down there below, but of course we couldn't get at them. And we'd taken out our party dresses.'

On the lovely Rambla, beneath the plane trees, golden leaves are already falling on the drinkers in the cafs. In one a telly shows the last dying bouts of a bull, down to its knees, dying slowly, slowly. A bus stops outside and people crowd to its windows to watch. The bull dies. The travellers climb back into the bus.

The telly next shows a beach scene, people bathing, playing guitars, singing. A tiny spot on the horizon turns into a tin zooming in jerkily out of the sky. It grows larger and larger

until it fills the screen. There is a flash, then the word Z A P A T-TELLI. The bus won't start again. The travellers pile out once more and push it until it does start.

The caf is the last place to which traffic can get. Behind it the narrow cobbled *calles* of Palma wind off in a maze. Here it is already night, beneath tall leaning noble buildings that almost meet overhead. Twelve grannies sit outside their doors on kitchen chairs. Five nuns pass, and a priest with six boys, holding a large cardboard box filled with pastries.

The huge open doors of churches show inside the distant glimmering of their candelabra and altars. Down a dark alley a notice says: 'Tea Pot 10 pts'. Next door: 'English Chips'. Then: 'English Beer'.

A steep staircase leads down into a vault.

The familiar sight of swilling pint glasses, familiar sound of British Saturday Night Pub Orgy, which here goes on every night.

Phil Gilbert, Eastbourne travel agent, dark grey shirt outside his grey flannel trousers: 'No, really, you see, I am torn in two directions. Eastbourne was always the place to which tourists went when they wanted something different and when they got tired of Eastbourne they came to Palma. But now I regret it. This is no longer Palma. I've actually just been on a tour of some likely holiday places in the Far East which I believe will be the venue of the future. In a few years the prices here will be too high. Looked at from the long-term perspective, this place has had it.'

Albert Rouse, civil servant from the same place: 'You could best explain us being here as a bit of a lark. We're very much the gay set in Eastbourne. Jimmy over there, he's in petrol. Jonathan's in display. I'm a civil servant for my sins. Jack's in oil, so that leaves Philip, and he arranged it. I know some people think Palma's old hat. Next year we plan to go to somewhere more exotic.'

He looks over to where Philip is pretending to be a bull,

49

charging the matador that hangs around the place to give it atmosphere. Philip returns: 'We've brought out a baby sitter with us, you see, a genuine Eastbourne baby-sitter, that's so the wives can go out and have a jolly good time. Unfortunately, tonight, you know how wives get, a little tensed up, it's the first night, well, tonight they mainly didn't come.'

'So we're all absolutely delighted.'

In another part of the stifling vault sit fourteen Yorkshire girls on benches along the walls, chanting Beatles numbers in low, lugubrious voices.

The Krarls, a beat group on holiday in the island, sit with pints of beer on the tables in front of them. Two eager youths in jeans and cowboy hats try to get talking with two of the girls, who wear close-fitting tweed costumes with broderie anglaise blouses. The beat group's leader watches them, then says: 'Drink up. I never chase after it here. I think it's humiliating if they won't offer it on a plate with decent trimmings. Why waste hours trying to chase it when it's so cheap to buy it. And good quality stuff.'

The girls gaze laconically up, not hearing, sing: 'Beoobiboobidoobah.'

The group leader, in branch-tight trousers, high heels and high short coat, breaks into song too: 'An old beer bottle, ten thousand miles from home . . .'

Four Spanish boys sing in four-part harmony an old *sarabanda* of Andalusia. They are only sporadically audible over the girls chanting 'Yea, Yea, Yea . . .'

The group leader staggers up the steps into the dark *calle*. It's late now. He feels blue, lost in the strange town. To encourage himself he yells: 'An old beer bottle . . .'

He staggers on, passing low doorways where hang olivewood ducks and tambourines painted with bullfights. He emerges into a desolate area where Gipsies are squatting on the earth in shacks made of old corrugated iron, sacks and driftwood. Here's a family living in a huge cardboard box. Bonfires. Naked children cluster round him, demanding pesetas. Somewhere near he can hear the sea. He turns back into the town, into the Calle Ecce Homo, crammed with tourists and the navies of six countries, and Spanish whores, splendid women, some of great age, in teenage costume, with great sagging bulging bellies under the horizontal pink and white and orange lines of their T-shirts. Some sober, wrinkled, in black, squat by doors playing cards. From bars flows music, not flamenco but American juke-box, the international music of love. 'I give you one hundred.' 'No two hundred.' From upstairs there comes the crying of a baby. Drunks clutch on to him: 'You want a woman?' 'You want ter see a fair belly?' 'You oughta try Barcelona. Bloke there with a spray, like in a hospital, going round spraying things. Lovely clean rooms they take you back there, sheets on the beds, flowers in vases, turn out the light, you know, all decent.' He staggers on, getting deeper into the winding *calles*. He sees a small plate-glass window: the travel agency that has arranged his holiday. Home at last! 'An old beer bottle . . .' he sings. With his sword he bangs a large hole through the glass. He climbs in, clambers over a pile of brochures, squats . . .

Next morning buses assemble, which then batter over the unsurfaced roads, raising clouds of dust behind them.

They come towards the end of the plain, and the mountains rear up ahead of them, and on a distant peak, at the end of mile after mile of hairpin bends leading up into areas that the buses still can't get to they can just detect a huge stone figure of Christ, gazing down with arms outstretched. The road goes on climbing. At last on an eminence overhead an old monastery comes into sight, its parapets laden with orange and lemon, and an ancient church with twin towers. It was in this place that Chopin and Georges Sand spent a winter together in the

51

1850s, and to them, their first tourists, the islanders behaved like savages.

The guide has a wispy moustache and wears tennis shoes. He leads them through the ancient church and into its cloisters. 'Now,' he begins, 'all the cells on this side have gardens overlooking a very nice landscape.'

They follow him into a small fetid chamber. Johnny Stogget, a man with a cine camera, a shock of shaven blond hair, pudgy blotched arms, his white shirt pockets bursting out like breasts with cigarette packages, bangs a wall: 'Hey, Mum! Look! Holloway has nothing on this!'

A Spanish photographer with a monkey face and in a dark brown suit approaches them: 'You like picture? You like picture taken?'

Outside in the lush garden stone pools are filled with water and coins: 'Hey, Mum, seen this?' Again he bangs the thick wall with his clenched fist: 'Well it seems solid anyway.'

The guide, holding up his hand for silence, announces: 'Now this is lock Chopin's hair. Very romantic souvenir. Here, here you know Death Mask Chopini. Very very romantic souvenir.'

They peer into a dark glass case, see a waxen mask, pale purple velvet, and a waxen hand coming out at an improbable angle.

One hour later, the heat is stifling. The little cells are so packed with tourists that it's almost impossible to move. So great has the crush become that a French group is giving the slow handclap to their guide. A second guide, a stumpy woman wearing a huge black dress, black glasses, and black plastic sandals, erupts through the crowd into the room like a tornado, yelling: 'Silence! Sois sage! Silence! Si vous ne tairez pas vous ne pouvez rien entendre.'

'My party, my party please!' desperately cries the man with the wispy moustache and tennis shoes. A German voice: 'Unsere Gruppe bitte! Meine Gruppe bitte.'

The guide, putting on a serious voice: 'Now, this is death-room Chopini. Chopini Death Room. This the original Death Room Chopini. You know, this the Chopini piano. Yes, this the original piano Chopini. Very very romantic souvenir.'

Eve Badget, Thurso boarding-house proprietress: 'Did you ever see that film about him? He died at the piano, see. His blood splashed over the keys and then he was done for. He died at work. Composing.'

They erupt onto a terrace succulent with cactus, clipped yew trees, poplars, and pools with goldfish in them.

'You going to take the fish, George?'

'Listen George, our party has been called for, you knew that, didn't you? Our party has been called for, George.'

They continue outside for a concert of folk music, given by musicians wearing dusters beneath their bowler hats, leather waistcoats, dirty white socks, and black leather shoes. There's a lot of springing, undulating, and stamping. On the walls are pictures of miracles and saints in heavy brown frames, and expensive looking oak chests heavily studded, and a blotched picture of the Judgement of Solomon, and Samson betrayed by Delilah.

They crowd into a bar which is in the form of a water wheel. They buy small mahogany pianos engraved with Chopin's face and which tinkle out 'Abendlied'.

Outside, three tourists pose for a photograph: 'Stand against that tree there. Now, look as if you were walking down the path.' Just as the woman is about to take the snapshot, the man unseen raises his own camera from his waist, and snaps her simultaneously. 'Hurrah! That was a double!'

Tables are laid under the trees, laden with expensive knick-knacks like small bits of wood carved like witches, back-scratchers, basketwork horses, logs of wood carved to look like Chopin, tambourines painted with bullfights.

Janice Portman of Grimsby: 'Of course, if you ask me, caviar is just a waste of time.'

Annette Webb: 'You know where George is? *There*. He took a short cut, and well he knows em.'

A French girl is rather scantily dressed, and a voice comments: 'In my opinion it's too high for the bikini, up here at 500 feet in the mountains.'

They continue to a 'Bloodless Bullfight', specially laid on for the British. Sitting on spindly iron chairs they drink small glasses of cheap white wine under palm trees, where an artificial stream passes beneath a rustic bridge and birds sing in cages attached to the palm trees.

There's an exhibition of flamenco dancing, in which the traditional grave face of the dancers is replaced by a smiling grimace.

They pass through the antique chambers of a palazzo, where hang musty pictures showing the last meeting of Louis XIV and his family on the night of his execution, the passage of Pope Pius VI through the Alps, 1799, the arrest of Pope Pius

VI by the French, and the Execution of Pope Pius VI. Trompe l'oeil clouds float on the ceiling over their heads. There are more damp mottled engravings and pictures of miracles and saints in dark brown frames.

Amid everlasting flowers made of shells and dried rose leaves, embossed in heavy gilt swags and curlicues, they come suddenly on a life-sized bleeding face of Christ.

Evening, the last evening.

The purple waves coming in along the long moon-shaped line of the shore. Deckchairs being stacked back inside at *Helados La Sirena*, and *Snack RENO's bar*. Evening, the last evening, and for once the heat haze lifts, and from the shore they can see the fantastic pinnacles and abysses and gorges of the surrounding mountains, which, during all these days, were hidden. At a little pinebranch booth on a bit of barren seamed rock over which the spray is breaking, figures, silhouetted, drinking their Coca-colas and Fantas at 15 pts a time, a man and a girl in each other's arms, another couple engaged.

Among the pines a small notice announces: 'A good cup of tea like Mum makes it.'

From the airport across the beach the cigar-shaped planes lurch like blunt arrows into the blue sky, one every two minutes, pointed towards the rainswept shores of Albion.

THE BILLINGDON STARLIGHT

A man books in at the reception desk at the foyer of the Biltmore-Hapsburg. Allotted a part of the Amethyst Suite, he follows a floorboy up in the lift. As they process along the long corridors, he is surprised to be hailed by a smiling floor-waiter dressed in tails. 'Ah, good evening Sir Robert, how are you? And how are the roses going sir? Grown any interesting new

breeds lately? Children all right, sir? What was it, Iain and Sabrina? Oh, very good, sir. Yes, I expect this will feel like old times to be back in your bed in the Amethyst Suite, sir. Any small thing I can do for you sir? Curtains darkened? Yes, done already. We know your tastes sir. Ah, here is a vase of roses, with the compliments of the management, not so good as the ones you grow back home sir, but none the less it comes with our sincere goodwill, sir, well yes, sir.'

How did he know? Fifty thousand people pass through the Biltmore-Hapsburg each year. Does he really remember the client through all these years, and his interest in roses? The secret lies in a room filled with card indexes, manned by four staff constantly, in an unfrequented part of the Hotel. The walls are lined with *Who's Who* and other reference books, and here in card indexes is listed the name of everyone who's ever stayed in the hotel, and everyone who's ever likely to.

Within moments of arrival, it's possible for the staff to be primed as to how many children a man has, when he was last here, which room he had, what his particular interests are – thus becoming 'synthetic friends' of the most authentic variety.

We continue our tour . . . through this collection of edifices through which the cooled air rushes like the sighing waves of the sea . . . of one, the Carrington, we learn that originally possessing its own gas station, it was the first to install gas-lifts.

The foyer of another hotel is decorated with marble and rosewood. A grand staircase around the core of the tower leads to the second-floor ballroom. A feature of the staircase is a tapestry 19 feet by 9 feet depicting the Spirit of Fun.

The Ballroom, designed to accommodate 3,000 banqueting guests, uses wood panelling and has rich reds and oranges in its carpeting, and a series of red and orange glass balls hang beneath the stucco dome.

'The International Restaurant' of this place serves, as its name indicates, a cuisine of international scope. It is equipped with reversible panels, sliding screens and variegated lighting effects, thus permitting creation of different moods and atmospheres. Menu presentations are, of course, attuned to these changes in decor, as are the uniforms of the waiters.

There is a realistically constructed indoor patio on the second floor, where traditional English teas are served.

All mattresses here measure 6 feet 8 inches compared to the normal length of 6 feet 3 inches.

BACKGROUND MUSIC operates in all public rooms and in passenger lifts, and is linked to guest-rooms through the radio receiver.

LARGE BALCONIES serve 23 of the guest-rooms and 46 small ones.

There are:

      63 double studio rooms

      60 single studio rooms

      42 double (French) bedrooms

      42 double studio parlours

      21 large suite living-rooms

      21 small parlours

      10 living-rooms

       1 dining-room and

       1 library.

ICE. Iced water is on tap in every bathroom in the hotel.

TAVERN. A modern interpretation of an Old English Tavern can be found in the basement.

After some hours spent in lofty chambers supported on stucco pillars, pasteboard arches, marble veneer stuffed with concrete, we arrive at one of the most superb of all such British edifices. Passing through its rose-tinted hushed salons we descend by way of a concealed door to the kitchen regions (what follows is a composite picture, based on various British Hotels, taking various characteristics from various places):

fetid holes, joined by labyrinthine dungeon-like corridors, stretching down beneath the glamour, floor after tortuous floor, stinking hot. Here the activity, the blazing heat of these airless floors that lie below the champagne and glitter, seems quite amazing, the hundred-odd chefs and commi chefs cooking in a sort of blind stupor.

Past a narrow Edwardian little chamber with a rack on the wall on which are written the names of innumerable chefs and assistant chefs, we travel on through a narrow door into a small room where the head chef is waiting to meet us, Emanuel Posauna, Maître Chef de Cuisine. He produces a bottle containing a rather heady concoction and pours out two glasses. 'I am always pleased to meet people concerned with the arts,' he says. 'We must be fair. The reason being, you make people happy in one way, and we chefs make them happy in another way.'

We squash past him along the narrow passage-like room, and he asks us to sit down. The sound of the kitchen comes distantly to us here.

He presses a bell, and a commi chef approaches through the narrow door carrying a bowl of salad and a tray with innumerable bottles. Posauna mentions: 'I am inventing this salad-dressing especially for you.'

The antique phone rings on the desk behind us. He scuffles past: 'Oh, good morning, my lady, good morning. What's that? Eh? Oh, you're depressed. I'm so sorry, my lady. Oh it's so gracious of you to say that, my lady. Oh, you are most kind, we must be fair . . . well, you are a wonderful gastronome yourself, my lady . . . so today you're depressed. Oh, I'm sorry. You'd like something plain. Yes, of course. Well, may I suggest some poultry, garnished, with some smoked salmon to start with? Oh, you are kind. Well, we try to keep it varied. I must be fair. Then to finish, quite plain again? What about raspberries and fraises du bois, you know, wild strawberries and peaches? With a little liqueur? Oh, you're too kind . . .'

He makes some notes on a card, rings the bell, and hands the card to an assistant.

'Oh yes,' he says, returning to his salad, 'I'm sorry to say the lady in question was rather depressed. Too bad. They have a lot of things on their mind, these top people. We must be fair. The clients they often ring me down, and they say, Chef, look, today I feel depressed, I feel this, I feel that, this particular lady on the fifth floor, I'm delighted to be able to say that she phones me down almost every single day that she's here to discuss the menu. She's a wonderful gastronome herself, which gives added pleasure. I make all sorts of suggestions to her, which, I must be fair, she usually accepts.

'The time before last time, it was a Sunday. It called for something special. We made a salmon trout and we made it look like a boat, and then we cooked it in wine and served it with a garnish. I must be fair, she phoned me down to thank me to say that it was absolutely out of this world. I said. "Credit goes to you as much as to me, my lady, it was your brainwave to create it." This is the sort of thing that goes on, you see, at a place like this. Hotels like this are hotels with a very much difference. The standard is beyond the beyond and they still want more. They are a legend. I think they may well go down as a big part of English history. We must be fair. And this lady, this wonderful gastronome, she is, I'm told, a very lovely lady. Immensely lovely. Of course we must be fair, regrettably I've never seen her, only once, for a moment, at the end of the main dining hall, I thought I saw, perhaps . . .'

What would such a man do in his holidays? Would he have holidays? 'I go to France. And I go and I stay at the best hotels that I can. We must be fair. And I always ask for the most intricate dishes, sometimes indeed very costly, we must be fair. But the thing is, this is one way that I learn. Not only shall I see the side that is cooking. But also the presentation. Here

I can pick up tips. And, whatever I feel that is wrong, in coming home I can see if it's wrong here too, and if so I put it right.'

'Sir?'

A young waiter tiptoes into the Damask Suite.

'Good morning, sir, a very fine morning sir, I'm glad to say, not too much rain, here are the morning papers sir, is there any other small thing I can do for you sir? Yes, of course. Some fresh orange juice? Kedgeree? Curtains open or shut sir? Run the bath? You were busy yesterday sir, weren't you. Yes, I noticed, most busy. Really, you should take time off. You should try to relax. Try to take some time off. Relax . . .'

In a subterranean office, amid a welter of hanging dinner jackets that he's been pressing, stands, iron in hand, one of the older valets. His gleaming dentures clack, soon he will speak:

The Valet: 'I've had dealings with quite a number of clients – Indian Princes, Maharajas, Overseas Prime Ministers, famous Film Stars, also, I am able to disclose, quite a representative section of the British aristocracy. Ah. We tell them by their funny ways. Not so much now. No, although they do still come. Not so much now, no. No. The aristocracy don't come here so much now as they used to.

'Most of the clients have got their own little characteristics. You know, funny ways. Well after all we've looked after them time and time again. You get to understand all their little familiar habits and ways. And once you have, I may mention, you soon get quite used to them, take no blind notice at all. Not a bit.

'At one time, I am able to disclose, I was personal valet to the Hon. Geoffrey Lawkins who was Lord Follett's youngest son, and stayed in quite a number of famous houses.

'It was quite a number of these places I used to go to. Oh yes.

'I used to stay in these places, as a personal valet to these various gentlemen I worked for. Oh yes. And so on.

'The gentlemen who come here as residents to this hotel get the same kind of service that they would get from their own personal valet. Oh yes. You go in to the gentleman in the morning and ascertain what he's likely to be wearing, and get it all ready, prepare his bath, and all the other little things that they'd like to have done, you see, their peculiar habits. Personally I go in to a gentleman and say, "Good morning sir."

'Now, as often as not, the gentleman replies: "Good morning Jones."

'What comes next? Well, I ask: "What will you be wearing today sir?"

' "So and so."

'Well, I mean, we've got to know more or less what he's going to wear *with* it, you see. Certain type of shirt? Certain type of tie? Certain type of socks? Shoes? And so on.

'Some of the other floor waiters here, I am able to disclose, keep a diary or a little notebook whereby they can jot down little peculiar things that the various clients might require. I've never done that. The reason being, I'm able to memorize it.

'Now, what to do if the client is in a talkative frame of mind, wants to have a chat? What is favourable to me is, I've travelled.

'I can converse with the clients about the places they themselves have been to. It leads up to quite an interesting conversation.'

The Hotel Policeman: 'Sometimes, most regrettably, clients have to be shielded from one of their own number. I've just had details of a fellow, appears to be going round hotels of this sort, smartly dressed, cavalry officer type, he's apt to talk rather big and ask his way to various suites as he goes along the corridors. He seems like a typical client of this hotel, a man of substance. Indeed, I believe that he is an ex public school boy. But that's not the sort of customer he is any more No. In fact, he's a criminal. Should you come across him, grab him.'

The foyer of the hotel is perhaps its heart. Here stand the hall porters, splendid in their peaked caps and long great-coats which they wear even in summer . . . here the head porter has his lair. The travel section of the hotel is located here, that can transport you anywhere from Cap Ferrat to Nassau.

And here too, lit by a spotlight, amid exuberant swaths and curlicues and sprigs of flowers, stands a young flower girl, one of the few of the staff not totally brainwashed.

The Flower Girl: 'Clients buy by price, not by name. They ring down and name a price. Five, six, seven pounds, flowers to that value.'

'People don't seem to get much pleasure from flowers here. I like it better really in the lower-class districts, where people actually get enjoyment out of flowers. When I worked on the edge of the Gorbals, you got the person coming in who would tell you their whole life story, why they wanted the flowers, who they're for, and what they did and where they worked and why they were very sick in hospital and how much joy they would get out of these six carnations; I loved all that. Occasionally I'd give away flowers, perhaps just a few half-dead flowers I'd give some old woman, she was so overpoweringly thankful. A person here just throws you down twenty pounds and says "Send me so and so." Often they can't even be bothered to give you a card to go in with the flowers, or even if they do enclose a card they can't think what to say on it because their whole desire is so insincere that it doesn't matter. They don't care. They just don't care. They just sling down the money and ask for a vase. They're distant. They're not real. They have no deep feeling. You can never get them to smile or be angry or anything. They order a wedding bouquet: they order it in the same tone as tomorrow they'll ask for something for their funeral.'

A small commotion: a bevy of debs and their delights

come sallying in through the foyer, bound for the third ball-room.

Maureen says: 'Specially the debs. People think they're happy I don't. I don't. They're sad. They know they can only live so long in this way. That's what gives them their pathos. They must have this money and this life. Which needs money to buy it. They're not willing to fall in love and start from the beginning, it's too big a step. They either back out of it before they start to be a deb, or they go through with it and become a deb, but by the time they're going through with it they're in with it for life. They're never going to back down, they're going to go on with it all their lives.

'When I'd just left school I used to dream of being a deb. The abundance of pretty flowers drew me to it for a start. It *is* a pretty thing, there are pretty flowers and pretty girls and pretty dresses and pretty hair-dos. But when you find out what sort of little artificial race it is . . .'

The man in charge of putting on balls is Arturo Jones, who also controls banqueting, dinner parties, cocktail parties, wedding receptions.

The Banqueting Manager: 'It all rests of course in inter-locking the various parties. Often we have ten a day processing through our various rooms. Some of the clients' demands are fairly exotic, obscure. We may be asked, for instance, to deck a room with lilies. Another party where we have to produce a highly exotic bird by the name of phallopeaea. Most most unusual fowl.

'On a great day, such as a wedding, this one day in a life-time, I try to produce something out of the hat . . . one trick I love to play is at weddings where we have a ball. The bride and groom are called by the toastmaster onto the floor. The band strikes up with a waltz. *Just* as they start to dance the whole room is pitched into darkness and on comes this tremendous spotlight to pick them up, this whooshing tremendous white spotlight, this has a tremendous effect. I mean, this really has a startling effect, one of sheer joy, you can hear it on everyone's lips, the sound of Gosh! How wonderful! How tremendous! Oo-o-oh!

'Interlocking parties can, of course, sometimes give trouble. Trouble when it does come is caused by delay, itself caused by clients, for instance the late arrival of some highly important guest of honour. This can be disastrous. The whole time schedule of interlocking parties is put back. Recently we had a reception, which was to follow a banquet. The banquet speaker was on his feet, most eloquent, everyone listening. He should really have finished at a quarter past two but at quarter past two he was still speaking, going at a steady pace. And at half past two he was still happy, still speaking quite content. And at twenty to three no sign at all of wanting to sit down. He was happy. A few coughs in the audience; people getting a little big edgy about getting back to the office, I think. And what about us? What are we going to do? Here we are, in the Viennese ballroom, all very well, and in this very same room, in what is now only half an hour we have another party starting, and here we are, we've still got these clients with us. One can't just go and usher them out, after all! He's still in the flow of his speech. We just don't do this! But what do we do? . . . I'll tell you. We pile up our resources *behind* the scenes, behind the green baize doors. Finally, just after quarter to three the speech does finish. The clients leave. The moment they're out we hit that room *so hard* with tremendous force of staff, that has been piling up all the time into twenty, thirty, forty . . . It must be stripped, re-set, re-ventilated. Housekeepers must clean, tablemen work in a fury because to put it mildly, we're *pressed*. In only twenty minutes the bride and groom will arrive. And the room, we hope, will look absolutely – well – only for them.

'Two years ago a client booked the Maid Marion's Parlour two years before the event to ensure that he got that particular room, on this particular day, for a ball – for the family. And then the unthinkable occurred. Twenty-four hours before the great event it so chanced that there blew up a tremendous rainstorm . . . a cloudburst, devastating gush of water. The technicalities of it I'm not altogether sure. All I know is, water in such great waves began to seep and rush through the room, and others as well, that soon it had inundated the whole of one floor of banqueting rooms and reception rooms in water, all over the carpets, vases, saturating the base of our pillars, carrying off the gilt chairs. With my heart in my mouth I telephone the client. I inform him. He says: 'Stay right there! I'll be along! Don't move!' Jumps into his car. Two and a half hours later he is here with his wife. Well, the first thing we do is to pacify them: Not to worry. *You* mustn't worry. *We* have got this worry, not you.

'With considerable manoeuvring and shuttling around we transfer this party into another room. This means a different kind of set-up, because the room we put it into is a much bigger room, we have to vary the lighting, vary the table plans, vary the flowers. Everything has to be changed.

'It happens sometimes, during a party a client will meet me and say how pleased he is that everything is going smoothly, and all his guests have said they're enjoying themselves tremendously, but he's then aware that there's another party, and yet another party going on, in the same department . . . and he says: "But how many parties have you got going on?" And I tell him: "Oh, five tonight. Five interlocking parties." And he is quite amazed at this . . . he says: "But are they all going absolutely?" If a party runs very very smoothly, as it should do, then this gives a feeling of great satisfaction. Everything is going click, click, you know . . . This gives me a feeling of joy, of happiness . . .'

The Head Waiter is the most authentic example of all of a synthetic friend. This Hotel has ten of them. They do no serving. Their job is to make the client feel at home.

A Head Waiter: 'I ask, "How many are you?" I say "Good evening, Nice to see you," all that sort of thing, then take them to the table. That's an art in itself. Give them the menu and then call the waiter to actually take the order. There's quite a lot in that, although you might not think it, every step counts. Quite an art in itself, there's quite a lot in it. You can't be shall I say sulky, you've got to receive the client, you know, make him welcome. If you rush up to them, you see them come in and you rush up to them and say "Good evening" (or whatever the case might be), "Good morning, Sir George" (whatever the name is), the client seems to appreciate that, that he is known, he is not a stranger. There's quite an art in that. Now what do you do if you don't know the name? Like this. I say *"It's very nice to see you. How are you? Good evening!"* and all that sort of thing. You have to use your judgement. There's quite a lot in that. "How long you going to be? This isn't one of your short visits, I hope, I am sure!" Or: "We like to have you here a bit longer than that." I must admit that there are some, just a few, that when you try to have this little conversation with them, well I can see that they for some reason or other close up, they don't like it. What do I do then? Well, of course, I don't. There's quite an art in that. I don't, you know, carry on, I just find an excuse, finish off my conversation, in short, I just leave them. There's quite an art in that.'

In a fetid vault an ancient glassman is straining to get the luncheon glasses washed up in time to be used in the evening.

An Ancient Glassman: 'I'm in my retiring stage, going on eighty-seven and I'd like to stop working but I feel if I did as though somehow I wouldn't be happy. So in my spare time I go into the glass pantry. I've been used to doing that and I like to go on doing that, I like the atmosphere, I like the way we carry out doing this certain job and I think it's a grand thing. We may have a banquet of five hundred, or even may have two or three banquets going together, that brings in a mighty lot of glasses.'

A Dispense Waiter: 'These banquets of a number of people, say four hundred, is always a problem, is always a headache, because that could well mean about three or four hundred different orders going on. Take twelve people at a table. There might be five different parties of the twelve on that particular table-order, and each order individually for their guest and themselves; each client wants the wine list. You get the amusing one who will say, What are we eating, waiter? You say, Chicken, he says, Oh, that's white wine. You take it to the next one, he says, Oh, we're eating chicken, oh that's red wine! Well this causes a certain amount of amusement! We know what's been laid down, we know what *should* be drunk.'

A Head Banquet Waiter: 'The secret is a little planning beforehand. You must draw up your charts, put key men in each room. You supplement these key men who are on the staff by the freelance waiters. These are the ones that you hire for a pound or thirty bob a night. They call them casual ducks. Sometimes we may have to draw casual ducks away from one function to supplement another. This is like a general on a battlefield.'

A Senior Barman: 'Long ago, when I took this job, banqueting was in its infancy. I took it on what we term the rough and smooth basis, according to the season. The rough is when you start work at nine o'clock in the morning doing *mise en place*, getting stock out, cutting lemon, preparing tomato juice, splitting ice, getting all the junk into the right rooms at the right times and at the right temperature, then the party starts at half past twelve and you carry on right through the lunch, serving, doing the bills, then *mise en place* again, more tomato juice, more ice, going on to a supper which finishes at four o'clock in the morning; this can go on a whole week where you're working eighteen hours a day. With the idea that, out of season, you could have the smooth days when you've got nothing. That's what we call the smooth part. We refer it to the sea. *Rough* is all pitch and toss, you're here, you're there, everywhere. *Smooth* is when you take your time, relax, have yourself in peace.'

A Plunger: 'Y'are the fella on the plunger. Those great pots are three feet across, the ones they do the vegetables in. Ya work in fantastic heat and grease. Ya wear nothing on ya. Ya get a great grease pan which has had chips in it, ya've got half an inch of chips on the wall, ya have to go at it with a paint scraper. There's no red in your hands, they're all white with the washing soda. Ya work like that for nine hours, and they're like slave traders. But if ya've got no cash and nowhere to sleep ya'll take it.'

A very old Glass Washer: 'In the kitchen where I work there's beetles and cockroaches. They crawl all over the food. One of these days they'll be crawling up the stairs. They won't be able to ignore them for ever. One of these days they'll be crawling into the bedrooms.'

Only one man at the hotel has been both sides of the green baize door: he's been both servant and client. This is a retired boxer who works in the lowest subterranean layer of all, operating a vast dish-washing machine.

This man is somewhat dim, and in the little room where he

works, criss-crossed with twisting pipes, the swarming Pakistanis have built a fairly well-known ritual interchange to engage him in:

'Tell him how much you used to earn in half an hour. Tell him how much you used to earn in half an hour. Go on, you tell him how much you used to earn yourself in half an hour.'

The man says, surly: 'Five thousand pounds.'

'Tee hee!' cry the Pakistanis. 'Now tell him. Tell him how much you earn in a week. Go on. Tell him how much now you can earn in a week.'

The man says, surly: 'Five pound a week. Five pound a week.'

'Tee hee!' cry the Pakistanis.

Music is striking up upstairs now, the night is beginning to come alive with the sensuous pump of swing. Hundreds, thousands of clients are streaming into the hotel as they do every night. A typical dinner and ball here can cost three thousand pounds. In a beautiful marbled room a group of debs are sitting on gilded chairs.

A Deb: 'I think rhythm to start with is the important factor. A gay, fast twisting sort of rhythm. And the band must look cheerful. If the leader or any of them look bored, it sort of carries on through the ballroom, or if they start off with a slow, smoochy music, you're bored before you ever get off the ground as it were, and then if they also turn out the lights you can't see any of your friends, you don't know who's there, everybody gets bored with the person they're with, you can't see where the person you *really* want to dance with is, you're stuck in the dark with someone too early on, and it's terrible if you can't see the person you really want.

'The band must keep on playing. If it stops for too long, then often something is lost, something you never get back again. I think the *ideal* band just follows the mood of the people there, at the beginning they're feeling gay so they probably want to dance quite lively and sort of twist, then later on if they see that people are rather tired, what I'm saying is that at three in the morning and the band begins to play a twist it can be rather dire.

'From a girl's point of view the least important thing about a deb ball is the food, because if one goes to a good party before, very often you don't want to eat, you haven't got time, you just don't feel like breakfast and the most enormous buffet from ten till three o'clock, you know, ham and tongue and everything, bacon and eggs and kedgeree. Most of the girls, they just take a drink and they hardly eat at all, they pick at strawberries and grapes. But the worst thing of all is – the smell. Yes, the smell

wafts through into the ballroom from the kitchens. Oh, it's *horrible* then. And sometimes the waiters look tired or bored...'

Far below, the staff are still at work, many of whom keep their whole families for years on the cost of one ball or dance function in the rooms up above.

A slight commotion in one of the long corridors as a packing-case edges down them, flanked strangely by four floor waiters.

Should a client be tactless enough to die he is not removed in a coffin as happens in humdrum places.

It might distress other clients if, returning from a late-night ball, they were confronted with a coffin lurching along one of the long corridors.

The hotel instead employs a large packing-case, large enough for a client, yet small enough for a lift.

Floor-waiters, even so, are alerted, so that it cannot come out till the corridors are clear.

The packing-case is edged out, down the corridor and through the staff entrance. Outside, the same tact is shown.

The packing-case is transported away in a simple van.

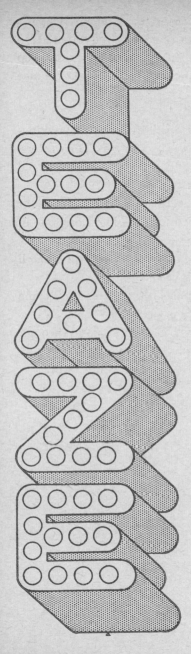

Soho today is intricate. It's the little rooms, squashed attics, vaults, and bedrooms and storerooms containing night-clubs containing bars containing restaurants containing strip-clubs containing kinky bra and button manufacturers, containing blue cinemas, sex boutiques, restaurants, shake-houses.

Soho today is that sad place that the bureaucrat sees one day when he looks past the Telly and his wife.

Now in the streets of modern Soho sex is replaced by substitute sex, the treat by the teaze, the honest whore by the parking meter, the clip-joint hostess in her spiritual falsies, the strip-girl with her little bag containing her outfit under her arm, her tottering little strides, her blue shrewd eyes.

In any age Soho has offered the British the reverse image of themselves. All that their dreams could create and their laws forbid.

The dreams today are wet dreams.

In the velvet dusk they push through the streets, the yobs from the suburbs and the blokes up from the provinces, the frayed night-loving crowds, in their smart ephemeral suitings, waiting, watching, pushing past along the pavement by the Whisky-a-Gogo, The Discotheque, The Kaleidoscope, The Scene, The Flamingo, The Ready Steady Go, crowding silently against the walls, into the cafs and the strip-clubs, standing for hours watching sleazy upstairs windows, waiting their turn.

A 35-year-old man is belting a woman around the face, spattering her with glassfuls of coke. She wanted to finish the game in which his stakes are lofty.

Two whores, slim, legs apart as whores' legs must be in their tight skirts, hair piled up so that they look like worried cockatoos, hobble off without note into the darkness, slow droll birds.

Groups of mods on their scooters sail in like fleets, their antler-like proliferation of chromium headlamps glimmering.

And everywhere, on every pavement, people waiting. Waiting. What for?

The Strip Club is down a narrow courtyard. Pay your ten bob and you're ushered into a small auditorium, heavy with smoke, stuffed with men, the centre supported by a large pillar. Men, as well as on chairs, are clustered along the wall. The grey line of their faces. A roomful of flesh. The curtains of the stage are all they should be – ruby in colour, in texture velvet. They draw back to show that the front of the stage has been barred. An exotic girl, poor thing, has been trapped behind it, tied by her leopard-skin bra to the bars. An amplified voice says: *'A fair young Jewish maiden. Victim of the cruel lusts of the Gestapo.'*

Music strikes up, music yearning and passionate in tempo. Then, suddenly, as if out of the blue, the crack of a whip. The girl winces. She slightly dislodges her bra. More lashes follow. Their virulence increases. With each lash she displays more of her snowy bosom. Now a new element: shouting. What can it be? Oh, yes, it is the Gestapo yelling as they inflict their punishment.

The music takes on a new tone, romantic, yearning. There is scarcely any break now between the lashes of the Gestapo. Other voices join in, possibly those of the management. Finally, a savage lunge, and the girl is free from the bars to which she is bound. The lustful shouting of the Gestapo becomes more bitter. A final cut, more cruel than all the rest, that sends her sprawling, prostrate. And now that both her bra and panties are drawn off her the poor girl lies naked on the floor. The curtains close. Some Enchanted Evening strikes up on the loudspeaker system. A few men get up to leave and others rush in to take their places. A voice says: *'Miss Lola Citrona. To see her anew is to see her as if for the first time.'* The curtains part once more. A new girl comes onto the stage...

We push our way back through the packed aisles, out through the foyer and into the London dusk. There is a queue outside now in the drab sodden evening, stretching away down the lines of star-spangled photographs of the lovelies inside. Then, as we stand there a moment, a tall girl with huge sprouting eyelashes confronts us. 'Hullo. You don't remember me.' She is really exotic. A vast mass of tawny hair cascades from a high bun down over her ears and forehead. Underneath she wears a huge flared thick orange skirt, and a bright red blouse. Her eyelashes are caked with black. So it is, of course, it is Joyce. Once when I went down to hear the pounding organ music of some pub in the East End, there again she had suddenly stood before me as I was talking to Gipsy Jim, the tall blond compère. She was different in some ways. Then her hair was deepest black, whereas now it's tawny. She says: 'Did you see the show? I don't only do strip here, I sing too in the nude, sometimes. Did you see me? I did that number half Alma Cogan, half Helen Shapiro, know the one I mean?' Her hair has one huge square of white in its otherwise tawny surface. 'That's the bottle style, it's like the highlight on a bottle. Know anyone what's got a lion by the way? I want a lion. That's what I'm looking for at the moment. Lions attract me. That's my ambition for the moment. Would be great in my act. I dream about them. Always dreaming about lions and snakes. Did you see my other spot in the show? I was the highwayman. You know, I hold up the pistol and then I say: "Stand and Deliver."'

'Joyce, are you still living with Gipsy Jim?'

'Oh no, I've left him. I did stay with him for some while, three years in all, actually. But now I'm on me own. I do still dream about Jim, actually. I'm still in a way involved with him. But I had to leave him. I got so restless.'

'Why did you feel restless?'

'I don't know. Sometimes I got to think myself that the answer would be children. But I can't have children. There's a certain disability in my family, my father and my sister are missing two toes on their right feet. And Jim had this wooden leg, like you see in the papers, if we'd had kids, they might have had wooden legs too. There's another thing. I wouldn't like to have children unless they're going to be rich. Money is important. People send chocolates sometimes to us girls, up to the green-room. Well, we're fairly contemptuous, Susie for instance, she says: "What, does he think he can have me for a bar of chocolate? That all he reckons I'm worth? If that's how he feels he'd better go and have a good work-out at the front of the show." Well, you see what I mean, I feel the same about children.'

NOTICE OUTSIDE, across the alley from the coffee bar: 'Now that it's June our girls are bustin' out all over.'

'Why did you look down when I looked at you then? You know, I think I have hypnotic eyes, because when I look at people they can't take their eyes from mine, but when I look down then they're all right. You're like that, I've noticed. He was good to me, Jim was. He was good to me, did all the washing up, all the cleaning. I didn't have any worries. But it's always the same with living with someone. Love doesn't exist. It's in the mind. He was a good spender. But, when all's said, I'd rather be a man's mistress than his wife.'

She sits, her long tortuous tawny hair clustered round her

lovely oval face, her voluptuous lips slightly parted, their pink colouring approximating roughly to their swelling contours.

'Only thing I don't like about this life is, well, sometimes you fall off the stage. Yes, the stage is too small, especially if you're doing a new number, it's easy to fall off. Then they've got yer. Grab yer ankle.'

Upstairs in the green-room the other girls lounge around, a lush sight, lovely girls in their drag, as they wait for their turn, the girl that plays the prisoner, the girl that plays the highwayman, the private secretary, the girl that plays the harmonium, the debutante, and the girl that plays with the statue of Napoleon. Their long lashes brush the air like antennae above their dark doe eyes.

'I was doing mirror before I went on holiday. But then when I came back I went on Napoleon.'

The intercom says: 'A shadowy figure . . . at dead of night . . . on the waterfront . . .'

Mary Queen of Scots: 'It's Harold that puts the tapes together, he's responsible for those exotic sound tracks. He joins up pop numbers with other effects that he gets from all over the place. Sometimes we have to restrain him a little, there's one point in the present show where he has all the fellas sitting in darkness for about two minutes while there's the sound of baths running out, it's meant to be seaside breakers.'

'What's the hardest thing about stripping?'

'The hardest thing is the G-string.'

'I think the hardest thing is, if you can't see the men. If there's too much smoke in the place, there's a haze, they're smoking too much. The reason being you got to look in their eyes. Otherwise you can't do it. You can't project.'

The voice over the intercom says: *'Miss Lola Citrona. To see her anew is to see her as if for the first time . . .'*

'Once I was in the number called Highwayman, and they had

a peculiar thing in the wings that you have to heat up, it makes smoke, for the shooting. So once I'd just got down to nude and got out the pistol. I pressed the trigger, they went to fire off the thing, but it wasn't hot enough, instead of smoke it came out warm oil, went all over me! The fellas went wild!'

The voice on the intercom says: '*A slave girl for Saudi-Arabia . . . Food for the mysterious lusts from the wanton East . . .*'

'He means East End' says Mary Queen of Scots, her voice an exotic mixture of Italian and cockney, youthful black hair falling round her face in fabulous cascades.

'The hardest thing is the Saturday evenings. And the Welsh are the worst. Frustrated on them mountains. That's the time you get them throwing things. And the souvenir hunters. As you take off your G-string they all make a grab for em. Throw them behind or they'll be in their pocket. And you got to keep away or they'll grab yer.'

'Yeah, that's the time sometimes you get depressed. That's when you get to hate it all, you go down the street, and all the day the market's there, and it's full of people, all gay, and then they begin to pack up, and that's when you begin to get that rotten atmosphere. The town begins to fill up with that frightening crowd. And you get to feel that maybe all the men in Britain are like that, all of them furtive and mean and impotent.'

The girl that plays the prisoner leaves the green-room, goes down the stairs, climbs on the stage of the strip-club. The stage manager is there to tie her by her bra to the bars. The cries of the Gestapo are warming up already. From the green-room we can hear the first lashes fall. 'Yes, that's the worst time of all. It can get you down then. You're on six times a day, ten minutes every two hours, it cuts into your life. Some girls get to feel degraded. It gets worse and worse every time you go on. Then the audience gets to feel it too. And that's the end for you. That's when you get that you can't project any more, you can't control them. And then they have no pity for you. The fellas show no compassion. That's when you take to the pills. And that's the time, you feel uninhibited then, you want to hug people, you want contact, above all you're happy.'

Notice, pinned to the door-jamb: Glamorous Young Spanish Artist's Model. Outside, the furtive men waiting on the pavement, cigarette ends glowing, waiting, waiting . . . I slouch up a decrepit creaking panelled staircase, paint peeling off it, past a sagging door saying 'Aphrodite Club'.

At the top of the staircase the door is opened by a girl in maid's uniform. Through it, vistas of an apartment got up like a dream set. At one end a huge bed with fleecy lacy coverings over it. The windows only allowing through a dim gentle light and in the centre, in a fleecy gown that half hides and half reveals, caught beneath her breasts to show their falling jut, an elderly lady. The negligee goes up to her neck to disguise where it has fallen into cavities and wrinkles.

Sound of soft Muzak piped in from somewhere.

The whore says: 'What did you want dear?'

'I wanted to draw the Spanish model.'

She puts her two hands behind her rump. 'That's me dear. That's not really what you wanted is it dear? For fifteen quid my dear you may do with me what you will.'

Says the maid aside, 'The blind one was here again.'

The blind man: 'I loved her. Then, when she went on the Game, I left her. Thought maybe she'd never loved me. Went off on me own, and, what was worse for me, I left me little boy with her, that's my Philip. So I lived all right without the two of them, and she took up with this fella, Dirty Jim. But he went off to nick for poncing, and one night I met her on the street what used to be her beat before the Act, and she told me little Philip was getting neglected because there was no one to

82

look after him in the time she was working. So I took to going to her place during holiday time, when Philip was back from school, so as to keep an eye on me lad. And I got close to him now, my boy, now he could speak, I got to love him. However the law got to hear about this, and one afternoon they came round and said if I persisted in going to the house where my son was, they'd have me for poncing. So then I stopped seeing my boy.'

'Step inside, gentlemen, the girls are completely naked on the stage, there's no hostesses to bother you and no drinks charge, these are genuine strip-teaze artists doing genuine continental strip-teaze, they are completely naked, I must emphasize this, no G-string worn in this establishment.'

Her voice has a metallic ring and it drones on interminably.

'Yes, they take off everything in front of your eyes, these eight lovely girls and they take off all their clothes – G-strings – nipple caps – the lot. These girls show you the lot. They stand before you naked. Nothing is hidden. The eight lovely girls hide nothing. We got girls here all varieties. White girls. Black girls. Continentals, all shapes and sizes and varieties . . . The reason being, variety is the spice of life. Ten bob. Thank you, sir . . .'

Her face is grey beneath the illuminated archway, its wrinkles lit by bright bulbs winking like traffic lights. Over her head a notice: '8 Artists Models 8'. She speaks in a monotone, grey, repetitive, unending. We pay our ten bob and step through the door beside her into darkness. Bricklined alley, open to the sky, daubed with scrawled graffiti. The raucous sounds of the street are faint behind us. We step on, avoiding a pair of dustbins. Continue up a creaking staircase. Through a door, into a close fetid room, and then, ahead, like navigation lights emerging from the darkness, a grey line of men's faces. We step down towards the faces, settling ourselves on a couple of creaking chairs. A curtain jerks back, and we see what we've paid out ten bob to have the privilege of gazing at – a malnourished young female in her birthday suit, one foot on a stool, her fleshy arse on a kitchen chair, a black wall daubed with white hand-palms behind, her palms on her waist slightly tautening her flat hanging breasts. Naked except for her tall black fur-topped crumpled PVC bootees. The men in the audience are pallid, detached, like medical students at an operation. Coyly she holds a hand over the junction of her legs, raising a finger every now and again, smiling with half her face. She coughs. She raises one arm, looks at her watch, flicks it back again. She clears her throat. A voice behind the curtain says: 'Got a nasty cough.' She snickers. Another voice chips in: 'Went down the slashhouse without her clothes.'

'We'll gather lilacs' emits from a loudspeaker on the wall. A buzzer sounds and the curtain slides back across. The men continue to gaze at the curtain, in silence. One reads the *Evening Standard*. A woman at the back standing behind the seats, a washed-out blonde in a yellow cardigan, comes round asking clients in turn to get up: 'Only, I just got a lovely dirty book just now, was going to have a lovely read, paid seven bob. Just let me see if you're sitting on it. Otherwise, someone must of nicked it.'

From behind the stage, a sizzling sound.

The curtain slides back again.

Same girl, new posture.

Just behind us are three oil salesmen, joking bravely among themselves: 'What lovely music isn't it?' 'Ought we to put in a sales report on this?' 'Do you come here often?'

A man with a haunted Frankensteinlike schoolmaster's face enters.

Three Chinese enter.

A self-possessed Negro enters: 'Oh, look what we have on the stage. Nice girls here. She from Notting Hill ent she? That's why they have riots at Notting Hill in those days when she left? Nice flesh, I'll say. And how!' He waggles his finger at her: 'Well, hullo fuzzy!'

The man with bald pate and schoolmaster's face stumps out. The sizzling behind the stage finishes.

Woman, inspiration of poets, artists, generals, philosophers, woman, flesh and sinew, ice-white displayed on the stage akimbo.

A voice behind the stage says: 'Yer egg's done.'

The posing girl says: 'Coming.'

The buzzer sounds, the curtain closes.

As we leave, the tout is still standing outside the door, enunciating in her lengthy grey voice: 'Now come along sirs, there are eight lovely girls here, they stand before you naked . . .'

She continues till her voice is drowned in the clamour of traffic: 'They stand before you naked. These girls hide nothing . . .'

We resolve not to be caught like this a second time, and we aren't. We're caught rather worse.

This time it is a young girl who stands ingratiatingly before us.

'Hullo,' she says, pertly, putting her hands behind her back and undulating with her stomach.

We stop and look her up and down. She wears rather dirty black tights and a frilly blouse, and her big eyes are caked with mascara.

'Were you by any chance looking for a nice time with two naughty girls?'

'What sort of a nice time?'

'Well, my dear, I don't mean picking daisies.'

'What do you mean?'

'Come in and see . . .'

Lisette says: 'Well, they have touts scattered all around London, some in Soho, some in Kensington, some down in the docks, everywhere. Their job is to rope in the clients, they promise anything to get you there, band, floorshow, the lot. So then they bring the mug up the stairs, and, we've got it all worked out, soon as he comes in you grab him, lead him to a seat round the wall. You say What's your name? Don't be scared! Then, when he's told you, you tell him yours. I mean, not your real one. Then, quick as a flash the next girl comes up: Would you care to buy the young lady a drink? Drinks is shandy for the men at 2s. 6d., and 17s. 6d. apple juice for the young lady. And you've got to drink it up as fast as you can, collect the sticks, and you get paid at the end. And you promise to sleep with him, promise him anything, provided you keep him drinking, that's what you're paid for, to keep him drinking. When you start you have feelings, you think, It's a bit low to do that to a fella. But you soon realize, if you have any feelings, you won't get anywhere in this game. Anyway, some of the hostesses is girls with little kiddies they have to look after back home, so they deserve to have the money. As well as getting you drinks, is these novelties and toys, fluffy poodles, plastic babies, potties. You have to say: Oo, how lovely, can I have one of those exquisite creatures? So then they buy one, and that's another five guineas. And after the evening's over you hand them back to the management and they put them back behind the drinks counter. And at the end of the night, for you that's another ten bob. You make arrangements to meet outside later around the corner. But you don't go: usually. Only sometimes some of the fellas they come back, beat you up.

'That's why some hostesses get such diabolic faces.'

Maureen says: 'There was a sort of wicker gate in the doorway and we had to stand behind this when trade was slack, to get the fellas to come in. As they used to go by, we used to have to gaze in their eyes and say out, Hullo, in that provocative manner, got up like art students we was. And as we was standing, you know, all sexy got up like students, as I say, artistic, Care for some fun? So he stops, asks, What? So we has to say: Do you by any chance *want* a girl? and he'd reply that he did and we'd tell him the price was £2 for half an hour or £3 for an hour, and this would usually get them, so next thing he was probably following me into the club, this was a little cellar room lit all pink and purples, with tables and chairs. Anyone that knew London would have recognized it at once, but the people who use these places are mainly provincials or foreigners and they don't know what London's like, they think that London's like other places abroad where for the same price you can *have* a girl. So I told him my place was just round the corner and he gave Sandra two pounds for a couple of drinks, and I suppose he thought as soon as we'd finished the drinks, we'd be going up to my flat, and of course he was wrong. As soon as he'd finished his orange juice Sandra comes marching in with some more. She's a fairly formidable girl, has hair piled up over the top of her head, so she looks tall, a bit like a monster, and very hypnotic eyes. And as she brings the second lot of drinks, she asks him for a further two pounds. So the fella explains that this was not what had been running through his mind, and that he considered it was time he and me went round the corner to my flat. So he got up and was trying to pull me out and I said not bloody likely and he tried to pull me out and then when he couldn't he smartly got up and did what most men don't – he went to the police.'

Oh the haze of the purple lights in her hair, her long antennae lashes, the sweet jut of her breasts, her sweet undulating voice: 'So then they got us into court. And the prosecutor there, he was a right lad, he really went for me, I don't understand it on my life, to this day, would I agree that my job was to get men to go to the room with me and buy expensive orange juice? was the way he put it, didn't I try to get them to think that they were going to get sexual intercourse? So I says, no, I don't. So he says, It started by you asking if he wanted a girl. How was he going to get a girl? I explained, Well he wanted my company. He says: O.K. fair enough, but when a man picks up a girl and the conversation goes, Do you want a girl? and How much, it must mean intercourse don't it? He says: I suppose men will go on being fools until this sort of thing is shown up. It's the foolish who suffer he said. Well, what you think I got then? Three months.'

Janice says: 'So then I went for a job in this restaurant and they told me, they said, the waitresses here get no pay. Neither do they get any commission on the food and drink that the customers buy, like you do in many places. The point for you of being a waitress here is solely and purely to meet the client and thus have a chance of getting to know him and when he's got to like and trust you you tell him how much you expect him to pay you in tips. Just for waiting on the fellas here, they said, is about a fiver, and for going with them after the show is about another fifteen. Some girls are greedy and try to put the price to £20 after 3 a.m. says the curious fellow that is interviewing us, but I think this is too much, so he said. Customers here are mainly middle-class fellas. They're ready to spend fifty pounds for a good evening out, but that fifty must include everything. Including sex.

'I tried a while on that lark. We used to take them the nosh, all just on the point, you know, sexy, then afterwards Mr Zaparella he was the manager (I don't think that was his real name, it was more a pseudonym) used to go up to them and ask them, Had they had a good meal. And they'd say Yes. And he'd say What they needed to make it a perfect end to the evening was some nice girls. Who are they? Well they're the kind you will like. You will really like them. Love them. The kind you will like. They will be yours for the night. You can take them home, these dollies, and you can cuddle them, play about with them, have a game, and they won't squeak. So then they'd pay their bill. At that place for twenty or thirty you could just about buy a plate of sandwiches, and a few bottles of champagne that the girls drank mainly because, although we didn't get paid on it, we only kept the job if we got the customers to drink. That price also included the so-called hostesses fee, although it didn't go to the hostess. Then we'd take em to the hotel that was near by, and book a couple of double rooms and then we'd all get into one room, in case there was any funny business, and there'd be the cry of Let's be naughty and we'd throw off our clothes.'

The Dancing Girl's Story

She is beautiful — wears a black fur coat, her face is very white and she has huge dark eyes in it. Her voice is refined, but with a touch of mid-Atlantic in it. It is a melodious voice, low and beautiful: 'My father used to torture my mother, I mean mentally. When I was seven, one day she slit his throat. She had to go to court and they knew it wasn't her fault, she was driven to it. After that, Mum and I were more happy. By the time I was sixteen we'd got to be pretty poor, and Mum saw an ad in the local papers saying there were girls wanted to audition to dance in a West End Night Club. She said: "Go along love. This might be the answer." The audition was in a very big dark old theatre. There were hundreds of girls there, girls of every sort, from the posh suburbs to the genuine mill girls. You can imagine the excitement. Everyone longing to be chosen. I thought to myself "I hope I'll make it." The choreographer showed us the steps she wanted us to do, and each of us had to get up in turn. The audition went on all that day. They selected a hundred, then fifty, then ten, finally the six of

us they wanted, and I was still among them. They brought us down to London, first class, and for the first few days we did nothing, just lounged about, in bubble baths, making idiotic phone messages to all and sundry because we didn't know anyone. It was like a dream really. And we didn't know anything. We didn't even know we were in the West End of London. And in those days we used to long to go to one place and one place only – Humphrey Lyttelton's Jazz Club at 100 Oxford Street. But we never were allowed to. Always, as soon as rehearsals were over, the closed car back home. After about six weeks I did my first show, and then I began to feel an old hand. Sometimes there'd be a conjurer there, and he'd be complaining about the size of his dressing-room like as not (as the dressing-rooms there were very small) and then sometimes the wallabies would escape, once they went tearing off across the stage and among the clients. We were really only like schoolgirls there. We didn't know what it was all about, sometimes someone would send back a drink or flowers or chocolate back to one of us, and then we'd all share it. We called it our finishing school, we didn't really know anyone or anything, we were unsophisticated. To give you an example, three of the girls that came down with me, for instance, were going out at that time with three Chinese boys in sports cars. We thought them the last word in chic. The green-room at the club was really green, but not velvet like it should be. Only poor man's green, or poor girl's green, imitation velvet. If we were in for the last show a moment after midnight we got fined. The phone rings and it's the boss: "Right, who's there?" So always, around midnight, there's a terrific rush of girls up to sign the book...
There was one very stupid girl, her name was Jock, and she was the only one in those days who showed her breasts, she had a beautiful figure like a Cranach, with very small breasts, but very white and pretty. And there was a law, in those days, that nudes couldn't move, so they had her sitting on a silver

90

paper and plywood moon and she used to sit at the back of one of our dancing numbers representing Venus. She always arrived late, she was one of the hostesses really, not one of the dancing girls, always resented having to leave the customers where she was earning good money, throwing off her evening dress and snapping the G-string between her legs, and she did really look lovely but when she opened her mouth you'd think you were in the Gorbals, she had a Jock voice you could cut with a hatchet. And she never liked the dancers, the hostesses never liked the dancers, they thought we didn't know the world, they never did like the dancing girls, they called us the Kensington Virgins. When she'd got settled on her moon, just before the curtain went up, one of the dancing girls used to call in a loud whisper: "Hey, Jock! You've forgotten your bra!" And she'd shout: "Help! Hey! Jeez!" covering her breasts with her hands, jumping up. Then she'd realize, and through the rest of the show she'd be cursing as she sat on her moon muttering under her breath, as we went prancing by, "Get away from me, get away, you scruffy little crowd of Kensington prancing virrrrgins!"

'We were, I don't really know how to put it, *innocent*. Once I was talking about this to a man and he said: That's nonsense. He said: This idea of Roedean girls doing P.T. and the happy parents applauding as though it was speech day, it's not accurate. The reality is different, he said. If a man is attracted by a girl doing P.T. on the stage then that means that he'd like to sleep with her. These girls may not know it, but what they're doing is, teazing the clients. He said: these drinks that you so gaily shared, what they really meant was that the men who sent them would like to meet the girl in question with a view to sleeping with her. Your friends, you were just teazing him. What do you think? I never knew what to think. But my view is, the men like it *because* there was no chance of it going further.

'When I first got the job I had two goals and two goals only, one was to improve myself and the other was making things better for Mum. I sent my first pay packet to her. With my second I bought a set of encyclopedias, and I was always reading them, in those days, picking up the education I'd missed. We got twenty a week to start with. Later it rose to thirty and forty. I had a chance to marry into the aristocracy later, but I didn't go through with it. I took up modelling. I was one of the most sought after of all Britain's models. Then I went into the madhouse.'

The place where she works is of greater opulence than the establishments that we've so far been frequenting. To the inducement of bared female flesh is added, we learn, that of the dance, coupled with food and wine. In a pinnacled building we call on the Proprietor of one such place, Mr Jonas, approaching him now up marble staircases and by means of antique lifts. A uniformed doorman in the vestibule. Bellpushes that glimmer golden. The door of the flat is opened by a spruce young girl, who nods curtly. She leads us forward through a fab apartment along passages whose walls, clothed in brown-sugar marble, are moulded into niches and archways. At one point a small coloured fountain splashes into a marble bowl. Marble then gives way to a sort of grotto-like proliferation of dark rounded pebbles and more fountains.

Then, lounged back on a white leather sofa by a window overlooking trees we are confronted by an expansive toad-like personage, richly decorated with chains, signet rings and watches, expensively dressed in cavalry twill coat and trousers.

Rising expansively to greet us he nods us to a seat on more white leather facing him. The room is filled with the heavy odour of orchids. Above him stretches the intricate detail of a post-Odeon Egyptian revival pediment and triglyph, executed once more in barley-sugar-coloured marble.

Handing us short cheroots from an amber box Jonas introduced us to the little girl: 'This is Tara, an Eskimo girl who has become my adopted daughter. Unfortunately she can't bid you welcome because she is dumb and also understands no English. Now I gather that you would like to learn more about the Club. The most important thing of the lot about it is, I think, the atmosphere, this sort of atmosphere, I could refer to it as the merging of the traditional values of British-country-house architecture (the sort of thing our clients are used to) with the virtues and charm of British girlhood, young flower-like girls. This brings relief, consolation. The people who come here are those who are seeking consolation; the major whose daughter just got herself pregnant; the city businessman who's just discovered that his son has blown the safe and pawned the family silver; the country squire whose wife just caught him in bed with the housekeeper; the entrepreneur that's just lost a fortune; in other words, it aims to assuage the costly but lavish sorrows of the rich.

'We have two sittings. At the first sitting there are always quite a few husbands and wives, husbands who've brought their wives along to show them it's all right. About midnight they move on and that's when the real night-club clientele begin to arrive, the chaps who've been to regimental dinners, the visiting firemen, etc., the fellows up from the hick towns come to set the place on fire. For many years now we've run the same advertisement, of course, bare-breasted girl shins up a Grecian column towards the sky. Clients just wouldn't like to see the thing altered. The decor too has seen little alteration; oak panelling, low lights, purple velvet drapes, the occasional chandelier. The reason is, again, that the type of client we get here, our clients seem to like it like that. The fact is, we cater for a certain class of clientele in this sort of joint, and they are the sort who will feel at home in this sort of ambiance. Also, these drapes and chands recall old times. To my honest belief, they were happier times.

'We choose the girls at auditions, bring them down here, wash them and polish them, teach them to walk and behave, rehearse them, then slowly we introduce them into the show. And, there's no denying it, it is exciting for them, exciting to sit out with the gents in robes, peers of the realm, kings, rajahs, and the ones in white hats. They take a bit of managing, mind you, and this, after a life time at it, I've managed to get quite good at. I think I may say that I understand them. I've been dealing with young ladies all my life and I can see their mind ticking. I can see their ideas being born before they have them even. Sometimes they come to me for advice. They say: So and so has asked me to pop into bed with him. I say something like, Darling, don't let that worry you! Just you pootle along, darling, do what you want. Whatever you do darling, I'll be right behind you! There are, of course, others who require rather the reverse. I have to give them a bit of a dressing down. I say: "Now that you're earning £30 or £40 a week you're getting ideas above your station. You're getting swollen-headed. You think that it's entirely due to you. But you're wrong. It's nothing to do with you. When I first brought you here you were just a mill girl. Remember? Well, stop the prima donna technique and remember the time when you went barefooted, not bare-breasted." My job is not an exacting job but it is tiring. It's tiring because, although they're lovely looking, our girls are often stupid. However much one may enjoy the beauty of a naked woman, and I enjoy it a lot, to train that beauty, make it do things, can be tiring. You may notice that I love beautiful things. This apartment, you may notice, is filled with flowers, beautiful things too. Beautiful in their way as young ladies. And flowers can't bite. A few of our girls may be said in a sense, unfortunately, to have fallen. In the case of most of our girls, however, they go upwards not downwards. We watch to see that they do. If you take an innocent girl and let her loose in London, she's in danger of falling. You've got to watch over her for quite a time, till she's ready to stand on her own feet. Once she's settled down she won't want to go to the wild joints of the potheads.

'One rather new aspect of the situation is the proliferation of third-class, tatty, or as I call them titty, joints. Yes, in these shows standards can get pretty low. I am at the present moment liaising with the assistant fire inspector to see whether we can't find some way of closing them down. Because, with our show, it is *not* pornographic. There are sixty young ladies, this is a high-class show, sixty young ladies that are so delightful that it hardly could be called pornographic. Of course they do show their breasts, but you see, it's all so young, so fresh, so flower-like, all fresh and gay and flower-like, all troubles forgotten, that, to my mind, the effect is more like a spring morning.'

'Not five minutes later and the brute had dragged poor Hildegarde into the typists pool on the 127th floor. She clutched at a box containing typewriter ribbons and these wound round the pretty little German girl's bottom, as, snarling savagely, the Swede began to tear off her clothes. She picked up a typewriter to hurl at him, but the machine was too heavy for her Pretty Little Arms, forcing her beneath its weight to the floor. Seeing this, the brute snorted in jubilation. She fought gamely, but Schnidkte, who had been a peasant in Saxony, was an ox and soon he was loving the little German girl . . .

'" . . . You're very cute. You make a girl feel kind of all bubbly." Her little tongue played around the inside of her lips. She thrust her hips forward and rolled them slightly. Sweat broke out once more on the Brute's face as he studied the rise and fall of her straining breasts . . .

'" . . . Grind me and groove me," she cried. The welt bit scars into her straining thighs. The rain fell hard now. Yeah, she had more curves than the New York State Highway that dame, the Brute reflected. And how. "Grind me and groove me," she repeated. By now the dame was moaning and turbulent with passion. She gasped: "You make me feel all bubbly!" Her little tongue played round the inside of her lips . . .'

Tempted by what we read in the hanging rack of the sex boutique, we approach it more closely – rub holes with our sleeves in the misty glass to see what lies inside, make peepways into the misty glass, revealing the faintly sodden goods between floppy covers, in cellophane packs, in tubes and boxes, the things to make us better . . . Harmid, the Great Restorer; Troglids, the waist and ankle reducer; Formula X, the sexational bust developer; Stout washable durable preventives (The Poor Man's Friend); and a device for adding inches to men . . . telephone numbers too scratched on peeling shreds of paper. 'Lovely Model has Large Chest for Sale'; 'Rainware fitted while you wait. Miss Belt'; 'Beds Made to Measure by Female Joiner'.

Further in, by the door, a textbook: 'Teach Yourself Massage! Boys! Give Me 10 Minutes a Day and I can Make you B-I-G.'

We prepare to penetrate the entrance to the boutique, that narrow door by which the magazines hang, leaning out against slack string: *Beautiful Britons, Sehnsucht, Spik, Delite, Teaze, Bizarre, Swank*.

We pass the threshold. A profusion of books now glitters before our eyes: *Love Me Now*; *Wild Nymphs*; *She Stopped at Nothing to Get Her Kicks*; *Sin Cove*; *Sex in Reverse*. There are also grave textbooks, written by lengthy German professors: *A History of Torture and of Death*. Perched among these a large notice in huge red letters: COSY UP WITH A KOZY BOOK.

A sort of ecstasy comes over us as we feel the heat from the electric wall heaters beating down on our heads, snuff the sodden smell of dust, feel at once fearful and yet excited, anxious to prolong our pleasure. More magazines here, articles on· subjects which, whatever else you might call them, could not be described as frivolous: *Fantastic Lust Plot of a Nazi Harlot Spy*; *Why I Treat My Wife Like a Prostitute*; *Can We Save the Doomed Pyromaniac Nudes of the Arena of Homer?*

For a moment our world reels. It is as if a bright mist hovers about us. There is a drowsy numbness about our legs.

Now we approach the darkened farther end of the boutique. It is partly screened by a bookcase, lit green from a discoloured skylight overhead, down to which the light must have come down a long well. The green glass is spattered with dirt, old orange-peel.

We look about us. The walls of this back room are daubed with patchy murals showing faded march hares with top hats, and carnations stuck nonchalantly into their fur. A man in a tweed suit with a seedy wide ferocious moustache is ensconced here.

We ask, in the phrase that we've been told we must use: 'Excuse me, do you by any chance have anything more interesting?'

'Interesting than what?'

'Well, than *Beautiful Britons, Sehnsucht, Spik,* all that sort of thing.'

'Ever had anything like that before?'

'Well, yes. But not here.'

The suited man scrutinizes us a moment, then swings open a card index on the desk: 'Yes. Thought so. Been here too before haven't you, sir? Was you the ones was interested in bestials? Yes, I remember. Well we got man and man, girl and girl, man alone, stallion, bestials, oh and a few multiples.'

'Well, what we actually had in mind was man and woman.'

'Oh yes.'

The proprietor flicks open a drawer. 'These are a pound for a packet of five. They're all wrapped in cellophane as you see, and the ones underneath are variations on the ones on top.'

Grey rigid flesh. Black hair.

We leaf through the man and woman section. Peer briefly at the men alone, standing sheepishly erect.

'Or would it be drawings you was interested in, sir?'

Also wrapped in cellophane he produces a series of roneo biro drawings, under the title *Henrietta and the Stormtroopers.*

'Used to be a knocking shop, this. Had two teenage girls in here. Try these.

'Else we can hire out books if you prefer.' He fingers *Torture and Death.*

After a pause he produces even more esoteric merchandise from ever remoter drawers and crannies. Gaunt women stripped wearing saddle and bridle: in thigh boots and nothing else: with donkeys: surrounded by flies: being pissed on by ten-year-old girls in firemen's trousers.

'These are of course a fairly costly item, of course. Supply and demand. Perhaps you'd care to glance at this. Yes, this is a set we're tolerably pleased with. In this case I produced the whole thing myself. Laid it all on – models, lighting, cameramen, the lot.'

He holds them under the light as we admire the complexity of curious positions displayed. As he flicks over to No. 7 he apologises: 'Here, as you see, one of the male models is unfortunately beginning to go a little soft. It's the difficult angles for the camera shots, of course. And it takes time. Heat of the spotlights. He got tired. You may notice in this next one, one of the males in the photo is wearing the same type of wristwatch as I'm wearing myself. Yes, I did, er, at one point, have to drop my role as director of proceedings and become, instead, an *actor* in the little drama.'

4 a.m. A man staggers out of the darkness. 'You looking for women? Yeah. Women are expensive though. Not many about. There's always complications. Don't want to trust the women round here, can give you diseases. You can't be too careful. Look, I'll be frank, shall I suck off your stick for a tanner?'

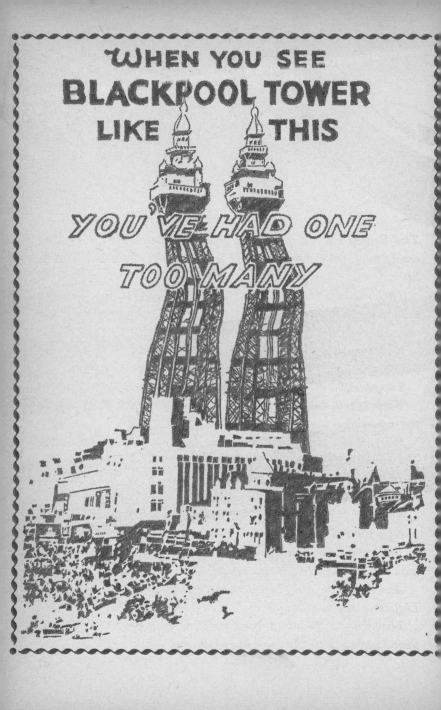

Seaside

The British wander along the shores of their country sucking candy floss. Or they lie propped in deckchairs, their feet deep in litter.

They remonstrate with their landladies on the rainy mornings to let them stay in after ten. But no, we've got to get the house clean.

Notice in the bathroom: 'Baths may not be taken without permission.'

They huddle in bus shelters, sheltering from the rain.

They spend their carefully earned shillings, all in a day, in the amusement arcade.

Where is the sea? ask the children, looking out across the acres and acres of mudflats.

There are Mums and Dads sitting out on the shore in their raincoats.

Spray is drifting in shivering clouds, in over the conveniences.

Now the swinging Scenic goes by, with its cargo of hysterics.

And now here come the ravers, tight wedged into their jeans, with bicycle chains in their pockets.

And the cuddle-hungry misses, all sweetly displayed outside the Laffeteria and the Tunnel of Love.

They wander, bemused along the floral mile of shrubberies, set their watches dutifully by the town clock.

There are cynical men in charge of this town, men who make their living from things like one-armed bandits and candy floss. People make money from these things. That's what one always forgets

Fred Parkins: 'Hello luv! It's you! Or is it? Is it you? Is it really you? No, it can't be. Is it really you? No, it can't be. Ee, aye, it is, ent it?'

Flattered, happy, the old lady says: 'Ee, aye, it's me.'

'But is it really you?'

'Ee, aye, it is, it's really me.'

'Well then, come in, luv, come and have a look round, what you going to do, you going to buy something or do you just fancy mooching around doing nothing?'

'Well, I just fancied looking around.'

'You mean old sod! Aren't you going to buy something then?'

'Well, I might buy some Rock.'

'That's better! What sort?'

'That sort that has the letters written on it. That's for me grandbairns.'

'Very good madam. We got all sorts of Rock. Vanilla, lemon, aniseed, seven types of flavour.'

'I'll have vanilla. Seven sticks.'

'That's more like it. But why not have seven different flavours, then you can compare them, the one with the next?'

'No, luv, because it's for me grandbairns, and if they have different, then they'll be falling out one with the other.'

Fred goes to get it. Over his head a notice says: '*Nites of Delite, Premium Novelty Arcade. Finest Selection of Buckets, Beach Balls, Spades, and Hats. At the keenest prices.*' In front of him the edging endless crowd along the promenade. Parents struggling along with squalling children. Then cars caught in a jam, bumper to bumper. Then the deckchairs, the deckchairs, the beach and the sea. Behind them and all round them are large badges saying 'Work Is The Curse Of The Drinking Classes': dark hats labelled '007': small plastic pots containing Latest Air Hostesses Of All Nations: stick-on notices saying Watch My Behind, Not Hers; Daleks; Spacemen; Dolls with Combable Hair; a girl inside a transparent pen with a notice that asks: 'Teaze Me. Turn Me Upside Down And Watch Startling Effect.'

Fred says: 'Apart from Rock, the old dears buy a lot of those little old charms with the Virgin Mary on it or something. That's their desire. The younger things, though, they want more of a joke. The best-selling jokes at the moment, I'd say, are the plastic ones. Big ears, long noses, Frankenstein monsters, smoking cigarettes, stink bombs, plastic kippers. Such like.'

He walks out to the veranda and stands just in out of the rain. The crowds still edge past outside like shoals of fishes.

'The biggest art on the front is getting the people to come to the stall, the more so when it's wet. What you do then is, pull the blind down in front of the shop and the people congregates underneath and shelters from the rain which is a sort of trap for them whereby you get talking to them and by talking to them you do business with them. You get friendly through a general conversation.'

He stops. He blanches. It is some nuns have just arrived under the veranda.

Then his professional manner returns: 'Good afternoon ladies, well, what can I get for you?'

One of the nuns says: 'We were looking for something that we could have a laugh.'

'Oh. Well, in what line ladies, had you in mind exactly? What sort of laugh? Because you see, we got any number of laughs, me lovelies. The Old Rock Sausages, Comic Postcards, and we've got these plastic kippers.'

They look at them all in some detail. Then the first nun says: 'I fall for the kippers.'

'Very well ladies. Anything else? No? I'll wrap it up for you. And now, ladies, I would be most interested to know what you plan to do with these plastic kippers.'

'Well, it's for a laugh. Some Friday morning we're going to put them out on the Mother Superior's plate.'

She looks trustingly up at Fred a moment: 'Do you think she'll laugh?'

A town like this (it's based on three different resorts) can seem like an ancient hag putting on her best airs for the troops: an affectation of youth and gaiety that is only skin-deep. With the arrival of June each year so will she trick herself out once again with plastic toads and dishes of whelks and notices saying 'Accommodation' and 'Vacancies' in the window, and funny hats that say 'Kiss Me!'

We begin our tour in the hinterland of scattered caravans and sodden pools of water edged with tall fences, amongst them rickety camp shops. We push on into landlady land, then on again to the amusement promenade, past snack bars selling super-whip ice-cream and jugs of tea for the beach: candy floss on sticks or in bags: fresh popcorn, cockles and mussels and crayfish.

There is the clicking of slot machines all round now. A pintable Derby, the names of whose horses are Sundew, Tulyar, Royal Tan, Quare Times, Pinza, Nickel Coin, Psidium. Next door 'Slick Chick'. This shows on its richly, deeply illumined glass headstand two girls in floppy bunny ears. Each holds a camera, each is photographing the other. Behind them there is a group of men singing, dressed in checked coats and boaters, clustered round a mike. Another man, sportily dressed in a red blazer, sits joyously at a table behind his glass of beer smiling, smiling. Radiant. There's a happy man. Smiling at what? At the girls? At some secret joke? Abruptly the smile fades from his face. The tablecloth becomes transparent. Inside the table a notice lights up, announcing severely GAME OVER.

What sort of person or power lies behind a show like this? We ask at the cash desk the white-overalled Irishman who gives change, pennies for shillings, and he doesn't reply, instead presses the button of an intercom and speaks into it. A booming hostile voice says: 'Tell them to come up.' We thread our way through the slot machines and the thronging crowds to the back of the arcade. Through a door. Up a rickety staircase and along a shoddy passage.

Then we are in a room of extreme opulence, whose floor is thick in pennies, threepenny bits, and sixpences, knee-high in them. Three brightly dressed young men are shovelling these into paper bags, watched by a stylishly dressed gold-haired girl of 25, and a small older man with the face of a dignified clown.

Sydney looks up a moment from the mountains of cash that he's shovelling. He says, sadly, 'It's right, Dad. All four of them losing.'

'Losing! And that's pretty hard in a slot machine! Pretty hard in a thousand-pound gimmick!'

Sydney: 'It's the kids. I loathe them. You see them coming along the front, heavy laden, their pockets loaded down with screwdrivers, spanners, so heavy their trousers are falling off with the weight. Then you see them going back, staggering under the weight of all the money and the swag they've picked up.'

He opens a small window in the side of the office, looking down on the ill-smelling clicking arcade below.

'Look at them. Ugh. You can tell they're up to something. See that furtive look of the face, looking behind, looking all round? Hm. Up to something. But what?'

'Ah, that's better. They're closing in on them now. That's better.'

A voice booms through on the intercom: 'Boss? Is that you? All right, we've got one!'

'Send him up!'

Later we speak to some of the attendants: 'You've got to cheat em. You got to. Take me. I'm working from nine one morning while one the next on a pound a day, well of course on that money I'm expected to fiddle. Boss told me, himself: "If there's young children that you can take advantage of just give em a bit of rock and don't say nothing. They expect you to fiddle." It is hard, mind, when people come in from Geordieland with their year's savings and you have to con them out of even the little bit they've got.'

'This place gets on my nerves. They're just clip-joints. The cafs serve up bad food. The trippers just get taken.'

'The people who own these stalls, the gifts what they get for playing the games, it isn't substantial to the money they put in it.'

'I'm getting out.'

'I'm staying. There's a future in short changing.'

A man swims out of the sea. He says 'There's peas out there. That Frozen Pea factory must have been dumping them. It's thick with em. I found myself swimming in a pea of seas. I mean a sea of peas. Look, they're sticking to me now.' He brushes off a few small clinging globules from his dowdy hirsute chest.

Town Hall Official: 'At the North we have the biggest Indoor Amusement Stadium in the country, a boon to the town because even here we sometimes have rain. Following this we have the Bazaars, Souvenir Shops, Oyster Bars. We come along then to the Pier Pavilion. We continue South then, passing the beautiful new promenade, the floodlit fountain, the new waterfall, the really outstanding Floral Displays. I think our Floral Displays must be some of the nicest in Britain, a real credit to our Parks Superintendant. We've got our own particular set piece which has become a tradition. Famous throughout the North. It's a girl holding up a bucket and of course the bucket is leaking. Established here for many years. In the summer of course she's lit up.'

Municipal Parks Superintendant: 'Our annual summer bedding out in the month of June runs to twenty thousand geraniums, about one hundred and fifty thousand annuals, and other plants such as fuchsias, begonias, and what we call in the trade dock plants, they are mostly plants you plant to give height to the bed and a bit of extra colours. We arrange em in a picture view. The main piece must have good edging. We feel like an artist, lay out our beds so that the finished product is like an artist's painting hung on the wall. The most popular flowers are the geraniums, antirrhinums, and dahlias. These flowers have such a striking colour that they attract the public and make them flock towards em. We do two

107

carpet-bedding displays each summer, one in the floral clock depicting high tide each day, and also a badge, last year we did the Olympic Games, this year it was the turn of the Toc H Itinerary.'

From a cracked wireless transmitter a voice announces: 'A nice cheap fish-and-chips meal being served in the caf. Don't forget to give your family a treat on the beach with a grease-proof bag. Freshly cooked meals served all day. No waiting.' It is almost dark. The cold sands are deserted. There is a slot machine near by with a black telephone in front of a mirror in a little varnished wood niche and written underneath: 'For a long conversation with a master of arts of Christ's College, Cambridge, put sixpence in slot, lift receiver.'

I lift the receiver and a voice says: 'I say I say, you know you really are an impetuous person! I say . . .'

Behind the smug façade of this town there lurks an uneasy conscience – as shown by the books in its shop windows: *The Divorcee: Strange Affair: The Claxon Girls: When the Lusting Began*. The Beauty Queen has been getting insulting phone-calls.

Along the front there are pensioners clustered in bus shelters, cowering out of the wind, pensioners setting their watches by the town clock, pensioners listening to the cackling of raucous little transistors, pensioners hoping that someone who is not a pensioner may stop to talk to them.

A threadbare staggering group of them is lurching its way along the promenade, jogging along in a dignified manner and at a steady pace. They chirp to one another as they go from shelters, seats, and boarding houses, others come out to join them. Some of them carry buckets in plastic bags; prizes won at bingo. The numbers increase until now there must be quite a score of them processing along the esplanade, and still there are more and more coming up to join them and the ones at the back are asking one another 'Where are we going? Do you know? You know where we're going? Where are they going?'

Finally, those in front look round, say 'Where are you all going then?'

'Well, we're following you.'

'But there's dozens of you.'

'Well, I don't know where you all think you're going.'

'I don't know where they're going.'

'They're following you.'

'Well, we were going for a little sit down by the floral clock, where were you all going?'

'We were following you.'

Charles Forgan of Wembley: 'The sort of people who come here don't want to just buy sunshine. They want something more than that. They can't get beer in Spain, they can't get British comedians, they can't get Punch and Judy. There's plenty who wouldn't want to swap all that in exchange for a few days' sunshine.'

An old man from Huddersfield: 'These boarding houses, these old boarding houses, oh, they could tell you a tale, with the piano going in the old days while midnight or one in the morning, holidaymakers out on the beach, paddling in the moonlight and the landlady cooking up fish that her husband had been out to catch. They'd be singing in those old front parlours till all hours. No more now. It's gone now. There's a new breed of landlady now: "Don't bring in sand. Don't be in after ten. Don't let your children play on the stairs. Don't have a bath. Use only cold water."'

Johnny Hardy from Scunthorpe: 'Time was you could see thirty trains a day put in at the station. Time was. Trippers swarming off them. Not now. They're living in the past here. They've been laid open to the slums of Sheffield and Barnsley too long. Now that they've come up in the world they don't want to come to this dump. It was symbolic when they chopped off the end of the pier. This place now is the last resort. What do we come for? Look at the buses, end to end, bumper to bumper, cars in their thousands. Parents trailing along with their kids in the rain, buying all that trash. Why do we come?'

A young man: 'I've been to Spain, and it wasn't very good really. It was in a funny part of the town. Well, we never got to the big city, we were in this little village. And we got picked up by the law. Walkin' on the beach early in the morning. About three in the morning. With two birds. That's all. And they didn't seem to like it, they just told us to get back into the town. It's a bit more friendly here. All the birds there they're chaperoned, that's a bad point about Spain. We liked the sun. Got plenty of that. Sizzled up! But we wanted to get back. For one thing the drink here it's a lot better.'

John Smith: 'Drab. It's a drab place. Completely drab. There's no features, nothing to lift it out of the rut. Is it a resort? Or is it just a place where the fish merchants retire and the litter collects in the summer, and the cars come to see the water? There's nothing. No Theatre, no Art Gallery. Nothing cultural at all. It's designed to make money from trippers. It's shabby genteel. It's drab. Drabness attracts me.'

A barman: 'I've been to Spain. The place is very well but the sun's too strong. The food didn't agree with me, stomach ache. I missed a pint of good beer. I'm not demanding. What I like best is a fortnight in somewhere like this place. This is my ideal, you might say. Get up in the morning, 'ave me breakfast, then two or three pints and a game of dominoes, then get me 'ead down in the afternoon, nice big 'igh tea, and then do the same at night. I've never seen no beer in Spain. Can't get no 'igh teas or dominoes . . .'

One Day out of Blighty

Andrew Maxwell of Rochester: 'Well, we come down every year, see, and we always come on this trip see. We catch the same boat every year, and when we get there we always go to the same place. They know us there. We have beer just like at home, and fish and chips . . .'

The ship's bar downstairs is gloomy and opulent, the floor curved like the world, with chairs chained to it. Charlie Speedwell: 'There's time to be passed in this ship. Time that at the moment's been wasted. What's yours? Here's my name for this ship: Floating Boozer. Terrific. This crossing to me, it's going to be a regular steady flow from bar to me.'

Bob Flintlock: 'I've heard a lot of stories about the insidious British tourist with his Union Jack tie and his ketchup. I'm not going to be like that. But I'm not going to just stand around. Oh no. I'm going to have a jolly good time in the way I know how to have a good time.'

A schoolmaster: 'Watch it over there. One cup of tea – five shillings. Watch it. And here's another point. You pay less if you're standing up than if you're sitting down. There's another dodge they have. The franc was devalued in 1960, but they still give you old stuff in your change. It's worth nothing.'

'What's it like on the other side?'

'Well, they tell me there's nothing there, but I don't know.'

An old man: 'Took twelve hours over this journey once. Hm. That was in the war. Expect we'll be quicker than that today. Hope so. Not the last war. The first war. Wanted to see the old Frogland again. There's a bus going out to the cemetery. Look up a few old friends.'

The First Mate: 'Last year, looking out the wheelhouse door, and there flying, also going towards England was a flamingo. So, that's the sort of thing that goes on. I understand that it later settled in the Isle of Sheppey.'

Jimmy Travers: 'I don't think they see a great deal of foreign parts just in one day. What they should do is to travel another day trip, this time to Calais.'

Frank Firley, waiter: 'Sometimes people make comparisons between the sort of food we serve here and the sort of food on the French ships that do the same journey. Really, there's no comparison. The standard on board the British vessel is far superior.'

'Most of the stuff comes from our own supplies, in Folkestone. So you see there can be no question about quality. We more or less treat complaints with contempt.'

'Well, look, that's a sell,' says Charlie Speedwell. 'Well, look at it, rather boring, there's nothing special about it at all, nothing special. I think it's bloody disappointing. For my money I could be entering the port of Hull from Lincolnshire.'

And so we process down the gang plank and onto the quai. And we are soon lost. We are absorbed into the mundane world of Frogland, scatter in twos and threes into the English Teashops, with their plate-glass windows advertising Welsh Rarebit and Egg and Chips.

A sign on the wall: 'The New Casino. Good taste and modern style will welcome visitors in magnificent public rooms offering the thrills of the boule, roulette and baccarat tables or the pleasure of dancing to famous bands.'

The Casino seems to be closed. Only a flapping notice pinned to its locked plate-glass doors shouts 'LUNA PARK. JEUX BOWLING FLIPPER BABY-FOOT DANC-ING.'

Mr and Mrs Alan Thomas of Streatham: 'We did wrong, see. When we came off the ship we should have turned right instead of left. By turning left we missed everything.

'No, we haven't wandered around much. You have to be careful. You might lose your way you see. I think that stops you. I mean I would really like to go and see the places of interest. Gardens. Memorial Gardens, Monuments, I'd like to see them you see. Items of municipal interest. Well you can't really go too far when you've got only a limited number of hours. And, as aforementioned, you might lose your way back to the ship.'

As we return to the catchpenny promenade by the old harbour I hear singing, British singing. There is an awning labelled Café des Anglais, and underneath it sit Charlie Speedwell and his butties. They're getting fairly drunk now, and a frowsty madame presents them with an immensely long bill.

And then the first mate blows the ship's hooter, it's time to get back on board, help! Some of the British matrons, thinking they're going to be late, are staggering frantically along the quai.

Charlie: 'Ultimately, finally, when I come to weigh it all up, my dictum is that, well, let's put it, they're not British. These people are very, very pleasant . . . very affable, very helpful, and quite frankly we enjoyed it immensely, *but they're not British*.'

The Old Man: 'Different to when I last came back. Took thirteen hours then.'

'I know. You told me. Did you get to the cemetery?'

'What? What? Oh, I told you did I? Told you me plans. Oh yes, yes. We got to the cemetery. Wanted to go see. There was one or two of my mates I wanted to see where they were, not them but where they layed in which graves.'

'I know. Did you find them?'

'I didn't. The place there, though, it's well kept. But I didn't find em. I did find one or two numbers fairly close. Tommy Metters. He died. I heard him die when he went across the wire. I won't forget that. It's funny to think of all them laying there. When I left em there I thought I'd do better than them. I didn't realize then did I, I thought by now I'd have more.'

SYNTHETIC FUN IS NEEDED

A woman grown through immersion in radioactive dust to a height of forty feet is in pursuit of her husband who, upset by her stature, has begun to two-time her, jitterbugging like crazy in the local dance hall with a mean blonde. There, as they jitter, she comes, this forty-foot woman, across the endless desert, howling, voice strangely amplified by the wide empty spaces, howling for her mate. Right up to the dance hall she comes. The skylight shatters, her great hand stretches in and picks up her erring husband and drags him out, while the others watch, hopeless, impotent. The mean blonde, abandoned, stamps her pretty foot in a rage. And so, cradling her husband, howling across the endless desert, wearing only a towel, the forty-foot woman sets off towards the distantly looming mountains. But her grief is destined to have an end. Before she's got far, she collides with an electric pylon, and blows herself up.

So, let us give thanks now for the stars, these women who set the pace for the world, deities of the flashing screen. They live on the level of Gods. They consume their life in caprice, do what they like. Beautiful, they bear their breasts like a straining burden. They guide lambs, leopards, lions on golden threads. They build heart-shaped pools. They ransack history, strewing their lawns with Roman pillars or 3rd-century Egyptian sarcophagi. Still, in the heart of the wild west, they change their gowns before each new scene. At Cannes they gambol in the outfits made from cellophane and fibre-glass to attract the

117

attention of passing directors. The forty-foot woman demonstrates their lives in allegory. Like her, stars are swelled by exposure to a size so vast that it befouls human relationships: the person is lost in the vastness of the image so that a natural relationship becomes impossible, exacts its ritual termination in death, as in the case of Marilyn, Belinda, Harlow . . .

The stars provide just one of the gorgeous images of the world we live in, the world of blunk. Now let us give thanks for other creatures so necessary for our times. Let us give thanks for the monster that Comes Out of the Swamp, the Werewolf, the Man with Slit-Ears, the Blob, the Vampire, Dr Jekyll, and Paranoiac. Let us be glad that these monsters are now coming closer to life, they no longer just skulk behind the celluloid. You can have monsters of your own. At a shop in Kensington they sell: hairy feet, luscious lips, smoochy lips, shrunken heads, bottles of liquid or congealed blood. One model is a half human's ordinary face with teeth, mouth, etc., but the other side is gruesome, with blood, scars, and the eyeball falling out. This one is known as 'Fallout', or, sometimes, just 'Horror'.

An actress: 'I went for this job and the man in the office he said, "Well, I'll be frank with you, it's a joke film, we don't expect a girl like you to take it seriously, it's a joke film, we can have a bit of a giggle, and the money's good." So I went back to my agent and she said, it's sixty pounds a day and I said I don't know whether or not to do it, maybe it will be bad for my image or something, what do you think, do you think I should do it? And she said, I've seen the script, and it's pretty lousy but it's not too bad. I think you should do it. So I said I'd do it.

'The first thing I saw when I got down there was the rushes for the day before. And there were lots of these prehistoric men they were running, running through a forest, and as they were running every now and again a vast hand would stretch down and would snatch them up. And they went on running, the others didn't seem to notice, just went on running, and we thought it seemed so funny, we were all laughing, and then the word went round – "Shh" because the director was watching, this was a big deal for him, and people said "Well he can't take this epic seriously?" and others said: "Well maybe he does."

'Then we went onto the sets and they were very beautiful, there was one that had a fabulous fountain gushing down, and the other one was a great arena, where the Queen lived. And we were all in skins, and these skins, a lot of them had been wearing so long what with the heat of the spotlights that they had got very smelly. The smell was overpowering. The first thing we had to do was a prehistoric dance. And most of the girls there they weren't actresses at all, they were hired from an agency that produces, like hostesses and suchlike. They were very beautiful. But they had to stand there and act as if they were humming the theme song and clap their hands in time, but these girls, they couldn't do it. They just seemed completely unable to do it. They took something like six hours to teach these cave-girls how to clap in time to the music.

'Then came the big scene. It was a fight between the Queen of the Prehistoric Women and me. And she came for me with a knife. In the script it said we had to get down on the sand and grovel, but she didn't want to do that, she thought it might damage her fabulous hairdo, didn't think about me of course, she said: "I think it would be better if I came for her with a knife."

'So she came for me with the knife. And what was bad for me was not so much the knife as the smell. All the others who were watching, they knew, and they were laughing. And I was backing away, and the smell was overpowering. Then there was this spit, and she was going to truss me up on this spit. Then she threw me onto the ground. And the director wouldn't let us stop, she tossed me around, and although there was sand on the ground it was concrete underneath, she hurled me down on the ground and I was all bleeding, I've got scars to this day. But she wouldn't do anything to help me. And there were nurses standing round, and the director wouldn't let us stop, he kept shouting: "Come on, come on!" So finally they trussed me up on the spit and, well, I hope the audience likes it.'

The tempestuous lives of the stars are mirrored in thousands of strip cartoons, in magazines like *Roxy*, *Marilyn*, *Romeo*, in which a boy meets a girl and there is a lot of kissing. Girls are jilted, they date, drink coffee, and at the end comes always that unexpected change that from now on will make everything all right. 'Suddenly' say the bubbles that come out of their mouths, 'the miracle had happened . . .' They've heard the glad message. They are in love.

Monsters grunt and collide beneath the kleig lamps. These are Britain's wrestlers. Three people became completely hooked. Six nights a week they travel all over Britain to witness it, travelling hundreds and often thousands of miles in a month.

A woman became addicted to *The Sound of Music* and saw it 700 times, twice a day, with a break for tea in between performances.

Let us now praise all those whose living comes from Holiday Camps, from Package Tours, from Cafs, from huge Hotels, from Cruises, from One-Armed Bandits, from Strip-clubs, from Amusement Arcades, from commercial radio, from horror films, from commercial telly, from pop singers and songs, from the juke-box, from musak, girlie mags, from lipsticks and all embellishments of the person, from films, from pornography.

Let us give thanks too for the pin-up, an especially pure form of synthetic fun. As she gazes from newspapers and from magazines devoted more and more to her she has created her own rose-coloured world of synthetic desire. How many have drowned their anguish between these coloured pages. A new refinement is to have several pages of girlie. In the first, small, she is clothed. Then the size of the pictures grows and she loses more and more of her clothes till at the end she stands alone, doublespread, or even with an additional bit of page that will let down to display her yet further.

Broiler chickens, reared in darkness, or in a subdued red light, should be drugged, and should inhabit a space of not more than one square foot per bird. They should be de-beaked to stop them eating one another.

Broiler cockerels should be castrated, to increase their size. Male Danish researchers, who first experimented with hormones used for this purpose, became sterile and grew breasts like women.

Eggs produced by the battery system should be laid by hens who live in small wire cages just large enough to hold them, and stay there, laying eggs, till such time as they don't lay enough or fall sick.

In the cellar of Louis Toussaud's waxworks in Blackpool there stands 'The Largest Collection of Anatomical Preparations in England, with one exception only, namely of the Royal College of Surgeons Museum'. The exhibits are described in the catalogue from which this is a shortened extract: 'Masturbation – This model represents the abdominal muscles of a man. Here you can see the aponeurosis muscles, also the oblique ring or aperture near the pubes where the spermatic vessels come out of the abdomen, and descend with the cremaster muscle into the scrotum. Particular attention should be directed to these parts. The first symptoms of weakness through practising onanism are here seen and felt; the spermatic cords elongate, and the blood vessels thicken and swell out sometimes to an enormous size . . .

'Syphilis case. The model of the head represents the final and most severe form of secondary symptoms with the palate lost, the bones of the nose nearly destroyed, and the whole system a perfect mass of corruption . . .

'Face of an old bachelor; a confirmed onanist He became idiotic and rapidly sank into second childhood . . .

'20 models of the human face – from infancy to old age – showing secondary symptoms of syphilis and gonorrhoea, in all its frightful forms . . .

'Onanism in man, showing the dreadful effects on the organ of generation. The scrotum cut open to show the state of the blood vessels; the elongation of the spermatic cord, through internal weakness; the cord being unable to hold up the testicle . . .'

Water is cascading down from rock to rock, foaming, splashing, endless. And lounging around and over a shiny car there are grouped elegant figures in evening dress, snuffing at cigarettes. The girl on the left, white clad, hair back-combed, is the innocent one. The blonde on the right, though young, is leering. Perhaps she's had more experience.

An ad-poet, describing how he wrote an ad for soap, says:

'I was trying to say that however loved and gorgeous you are, B.O. is something you share with all women, but that if you accept this, accept your body for what it is by using this soap, you can feel as fresh and cool as this model.'

Many ad-poets are inspired by the *automobile*. When they launched the Consul Classic, Ford held a series of midnight parties. At places like Reading there were cars parked for miles. 250,000 people came to these parties. It was this sort of scene that inspired an ad-poet to write the following lyric:

> Take a long look at the long low look,
> set the style,
> make the pace
> with the all-new Consul Classic from Ford.

One recent Sunday, not a Bank Holiday, there was a queue of motors eighteen miles long.

Twenty people are killed and a thousand injured by cars each day. Four thousand people were killed in the first seven months of last year, and 55,000 badly hurt.

A man: 'I am out in the open country. There is a someone sitting beside me. She is fascinated by the way I drive the car in this world of low-flung cloud and heather. Oh yes, there's an accident. Accidents make the journey seem better, exciting. And now we're taking to the ocean. Sunday dinner is cooking in the oven behind us and now, as the sun sets over the ocean, the seats let down, and me and that Special Someone are bedded down together as the spray flies and our speed approaches 100 m.p.h.'

Let us give thanks now for the *Telly*, of all synthetic fun purveyors perhaps the greatest. Its array of synthetic friends with their glittering black-and-white smiles, its endless quizzes and parlour games, introduce us into a fragile and seductive world. It should be watched on every possible occasion. From an ad: 'Ever wished you could carry on viewing – in bed – in your kitchen – in the den? Well now you can. Want an early night? Don't want to miss your favourite programme? Then up to bed with the Carry-Telly, for continuous performance. Painting to do? Carpentry to finish? Television you'd love to see? Then carry on viewing with the wonderful new Carry Telly that you simply pick up, plug in and switch on wherever you want it.'

A lady in Liverpool is so addicted to the telly that she sits waiting an hour or so before it begins, including programmes in the Welsh tongue when she can get them. She watches through to the end of night, and, should anyone interrupt, sometimes becomes so angry that she resorts to violence. An old woman tells me: 'When the man on the Telly says goodnight, that's when I feel so close to him, so happy, I feel I needn't worry no more.'

Bearded, long-haired and wearing tight pantaloons and knee-length boots and sporting a large gold-coloured brooch at his neck, a free-lance writer caused consternation in Edith Grove, Chelsea, by firing a cap pistol at passers-by. Caught after a chase, he was found to have a sheath-knife slung at his hip and he told a police officer: 'I am Amos Burke.'

Viewers put vases of flowers on the set over the heads of those they adore. Or, noticing that their favourite Newscaster has a sore throat, place there a glass of cough medicine.

The radio has its share of this too. Sunday afternoon sees motorists scouring the shires to discover Ambridge, the fictional village where the Archers' farm is.

And when Dan Archer once mentioned that he was thinking of taking on a new farm labourer, there were hundreds of letters applying for the job. It is said that some even called in person, came up all hot after milking, just as they were, to the foyer of Broadcasting House.

Advertisers on the Telly have various manuals to dictate good taste.

Toilet Cleansers: Demonstrations of toilet cleansers must not show a shot of a lavatory pan, but a toilet cleanser may be shown on a bathroom window ledge or being held above the actual toilet. This should not reveal any part of the toilet itself.

Toilet Paper: Care should be taken when showing toilet rolls. They should not be shown installed.

Synthetic fun and other projects already take up a fifth of our coastline. The coast is now disappearing at the rate of five miles a year. At present rate of acceleration this will soon use it all up. Then Britain will be a 'vast caravan-park-cum-litter-scape-cum-traffic-jam.'

A fanfare . . . then a voice says: 'Here Here! Alice in Wonderland invites you to enjoy her adventures.' The amplified voice of Alice says: 'How exciting Wonderland is. I know you have always wanted to see the lovely land yourself. And more. My

125

wonderful friends have come to life in this Castle. Step forward then my loyal friends. There's welcome and fun inside for my loyal friends of all ages. Welcome and enjoy yourselves. If you can ride a Cheshire cat your wonderful adventure will begin. Come now, old and young, be *gay* in Wonderland.'

The plastic carriage rides through an arch hung with plastic leaves and into darkness. Then, in turn, Alice's friends spring into life, odd animals that leap up, go Pfff! And then vanish. Chairs revolve. Then the carriage arrives at the centre-piece – a twenty-foot-high figure of Alice, swaying an exotic purple hockey stick between her legs. But this lovely schoolgirl apparition alas has been violated. Oh dear. Most foully. For this girl has no head. Only darkness where her lovely chin and her lips and eyes and blonde tresses should be. The head is gone.

Outside Blackpool a bus waits in a jam. Then slowly it crawls forward again, slowly towards the coastline. Again it is stuck in a jam. And the black sea is in front, the road gives a turn, and there is the great arch astride the road, that great yet squashed streamlined arch, pink, yellow, and purple, with the proud words in blue, and then, in red and white, 'ALWAYS WELCOME'. The cars now are totally packed, four abreast. It will take us six hours to cover the six golden miles of the illuminations seen each year by eight million people.

The golden arches stretch away into the dusk, and giant stylized trees whose branches bear plastic roses and yellow baskets filled with these same glimmering plastic roses. If ever there may be a National Mecca for all our folklore it must be here, wheelborne, in the dark night amidst exhaust fumes, in a bus, or best in your own car, caught in a ritual traffic jam. All around you other people, together yet alone, in *their* status settings. A good run for the car in *your* life, why not try it? And meanwhile to keep you delighted there drifts past in turn a conspectus of our various National symbols, those bright

126

images by which we live, culled from the world of nursery rhymes, fairy tales, space travel, pantomime, religion, telly. By now the speed is one mile an hour. It will take up to seven hours to get to the end of the six-mile display.

The motif of plastic trees and roses that has been with us overhead changes. Now it is musicians, zylophonists, black and white minstrels, kettle-drum players. A series called 'Valentine Memories' follows, with bulbous plastic illuminated yellow cherubs. Tavern Tales follow, sculptured figures in jack-boots with glasses of port, footloose serving boys, red-nosed ostlers, sexy serving wenches. Astraland, with zooming rockets and space travellers. Snow White and the Seven Dwarfs. Goldilocks and the Three Bears. Alice in Wonderland ... And finally the famous Tower stretches above us, lit with its thousands and thousands of glimmering bulbs, reflected in the restless sea.

Municipal trams pass, lit up with thousands of lights: a rocket, yellow pink, pointing up as if to launch into the stratosphere. A ship unexpectedly emblazoned 'Prudential Assurance'. An old-fashioned tram ablaze with white, blue, and yellow. In the light of these spirited trams the faces of children in passing cars are lit brightly in wonder, and mothers pointing out to their children fresh delights to look at ...

Let us give thanks for the open road, as we continue to crawl round this spoiled countryside in our tin beetles. Finding one beach packed, we will continue to the next beach and the next and the next. In the next fifty years the land in urban use will increase by two million acres. Not long now and what we think of as countryside will all be gone. Perhaps we should not care. Perhaps there will then be less anguish. Better a ravished woman than the act of violation constantly before our eyes. Anyway, we can't complain. We're as guilty as the next man. In our need for synthetic fun to lull us we are a part of this violation.

One agency offers a very special evening's *synthetic friendship*. Typical among the girls on offer is 'MAVIS, age 22. Indeed a vivacious and fascinating companion with a sweet disposition. Mavis's main interests are ballet and the theatre.' An evening's instant romance with Mavis will cost you eight guineas, four for the firm and four for the girl. If it's a business

function you have in mind the girl will be happy to pretend that she is your 'friend'. Only you will know that it is a rule of the firm that it should be 'clean' instant friendship.

In our lunatic asylums men sleep in dormitories for up to sixty. In our doss-houses the human detritus of an age congregate like litter, and they sleep in dormitories of up to eighty.

Synthetic fun is needed.

The Reception Bunny smiles at you as you enter. Her smile is rehearsed: the 'Bunny Book' tells her that she must 'ESTABLISH A FRIENDLY RELATIONSHIP WITH A GENUINE SMILE AND GOOD EYE CONTACT.' Your entry into the building is relayed throughout the various bars and salons on closed-circuit television. You stop to chat a moment with 'The Polaroid Bunny' all ready to snap you, toy with the idea of a game of billiards with the 'Pool Bunny'.

The Bunnies, 'good girls dressed up to look like bad girls', wear tight one-piece swimsuit-style garments, in black or red, boned, often stuffed with handkerchiefs forcing the breasts up above their top. These are the ideal instant girl friend, pin-ups made flesh. You may see, smell and hear them, but may not touch or taste. They are the musak of love. They wear floppy sows ears, a white collar round their naked necks, a small black bow tie, and white cuffs with links on their sleeveless arms. If you pinch a Bunny's behind, she'll say: 'Excuse me sir, you're not supposed to touch Bunnies.' Other reactions to you may be a thing called the 'Bunny Dip' and the greeting: 'Good Evening, Sir, I am your Bunny, Dolly.' To make sure that she is neither touching nor dating clients, the club hires an agency which sends men along to 'test the merit and mettle' of Bunnies, men 'experienced in creating situations that will tempt the unwary to violate rules'.

A Bunny may not drink anything, even water, in view of guests. The reason for this is that clients can't tell whether she's drinking water or gin. They might get the impression –

and it might well be an understandable one – that she is getting quietly stoned.

The Tour Director stands in a large dark vault. Around stretch the blue buses, huddled together like whales in an underwater tank. To the raincoated tourists approaching he says: 'Yes sir. Rural England? Yes sir. Stately Homes? This way, sir. Coach 4B for the Cathedrals, madam. Ancient and Modern, Number Seven. What's that madam? Stone Hedge? Ah, yes, this way please madam.'

He's a neat man, balding, one lock curled across the pink back of his scalp, the rest of his grey hair being closely cropped. His suit is pinstriped, dark blue, shabby. He wears black shiny galoshes over his brown serge shoes. Now his own tour, to the 'Shakespeare country' is due to depart, most popular of all tours of Britain's Heritage, known in the trade as the 'Rat Run'.

He climbs in, sinks back into the front seat of the coach, a seat with a cleft down the middle, red, pink and white scrolls and swirls, and a shiny white plastic headrest. Hot air is blowing through a vent in the floor, warming his galoshes. Now he picks up a small microphone, hears his voice trickle down through amber grilles in between the orange skylights behind him. The driver revs up, the coach shudders and vibrates, we're off.

' . . . In addition to visiting the Birthroom of Shakespeare and Anne Hathaway's cottage, and in order to give a more varied interest to the 220-mile journey, we're going to visit one or two other places. But before I mention what they are, you might like to have a look on the left at the medical quarter – Harley Street – quite a famous name in medical circles . . . also, you may notice Wimpole Street, home of the Barrett Brownings . . .'

He sits thrown back into his upholstered seat, as if by violent impact. When speaking, his voice has a way of trailing up at the end as if he couldn't quite hold on to it: ' . . . We'll have refreshment breaks of course, otherwise it's rather a long day. We'll have a proper luncheon at Warwick . . . By the way, during the ride, you'll have time for your gossips and snoozes . . .'

In front of him there are nosegays of plastic roses attached to the windscreen. He snatches a moment to read to himself from a small battered volume. The road becomes more open. We pass decrepit gipsy caravans, abandoned cars, sodden windblown groups waiting by bus stops, their polythene macintoshes fluttering – not part of Britain's Heritage. He looks up from his book: ' . . . On your right you will see now the pleasant eighteenth-century butter cross of High Wycombe.' He avoids mentioning a placard leaning against it announcing 'The Krarls! the most blues-wailing, they're gear, they're fab!' – not part of Britain's Heritage.

An hour or so later, after a break to drink coffee and biscuits in a shoddy canteen, we arrive at ' . . . Oxford . . . generally accepted to be the oldest British University . . . The sexes mingle freely together in their studies . . . there are quite a number of sports and games . . .

' . . . Now leaving Oxford in a northerly direction, we set off for Warwick. Quite a pleasant drive . . .

' . . . Blenheim. This is on our left now. You can maybe see the wall, eight miles long, enclosing a park of some twenty-five thousand acres . . .

' . . . Now here we are in Warwick. We're entering the town by the West Gate. Later, the other side of the town, we'll be leaving by the East Gate . . .'

He leads us through the rain to lunch on curried broiler chicken, soup, ice-cream and water. Then he creeps along at our head down a gorge till the castle appears before us. He says: 'By the way, I should perhaps point out in all fairness that the guide is blind.'

The blind guide standing in an ornate vault says: 'This chapel is used for the family's private devotions. The Picture on the right is by Ferrucino – note the lovely colouring. There is an alabaster vase, this was filled last time with arum lilies . . . A picture of David, Lord Brooke, when he was a boy at Eton . . . again, note the lovely colouring.'

We enter a room full of vast shields, and a stuffed bear.

The Tour Director, banging a tall gilt frame decorated with carved drums, swags and trumpets, says: 'This frame is very heavy, they say. Hard to dust I'd say too. The armour is actually mainly family armour. The small door at the far end is important. It leads to the private family apartments. While you're here, you might like to glance briefly down the gorge here, at the lovely river flowing far underneath us.'

The surface of the river far below is ribbed with small mountains of detergent.

'And now for the high spot of our tour, Stratford-upon-Avon . . .'

The bus pulls up at the end of a long queue of similar buses outside a nondescript half-timbered house. We enter a low, airless apartment.

A man with loud, monotonous voice, blue suit, Brylcreemed hair and striped tie announces: 'Here the third child of John Shakespeare was born in 1564. Upstairs you'll find the Birth-room.'

The Tour Director: 'Very much restored, in fact, but of historic importance. The actual house of Shakespeare no longer exists, so this is of increased historic importance, naturally. There are toilets and rest-rooms in the rear of the premises, incidentally.'

We pass through the empty dun-coloured rooms, viewing 'an early wrought iron pin', 'fragments of an old comb', and copies of the few relics of the mysterious William Shakespeare.

The Tour Director: 'Shakespeare's daughter lived over

there . . . the one that's now a Wimpey Bar. They do have a tomb that is shown as William Shakespeare's, but it's thought to be spurious. They celebrate his birthday on April 23rd, but of course that is conjecture . . .'

The sun has come out now. We continue through the sweltering town, through subtopia.

Again we crowd into a minute half-timbered cottage.

A large woman in dark blue costume addresses us: 'Hullo, ladies and gents, I'm sorry that my voice has gone, I've had a busy year, I hope you can hear me. Now this is the farmhouse occupied by the family of Shakespeare's wife, Anne Hathaway. Upstairs the famous Hathaway bed will show you how they slept in those days. Amongst you, you may note the famous settle where William sat and courted his Anne. Now as you proceed upstairs you may find that some steps are not where they're meant to be, also the ceiling is rather low. So watch both ends.'

the glass coach . . .
there 𝖘𝖍𝖊 is for the first time. 𝖘𝖍𝖊 is devastatingly beautiful . . .
from the extreme top right hand corner of our window frame we can see now . . .
one magnificent moment which was however but a prelude . . .
shining in the sunlight they swing left now . . .
crowd of girl guides . . .
ladies in waiting . . .
yes there 𝖘𝖍𝖊 is . . .
turquoise blue . . .
hardly a breath of breeze now to flutter the union jacks . . .
troops of stalwart life-guards . . .
this is the moment . . .
some waiting some hours now . . .
flash of whiteness inside the coach
𝖞𝖊𝖘!

Members of the teenscene in their fabulous plumage which they buy one week only to discard the next or the next, with their scooters hung with status-giving gimmicks, with their paper clothes, their ephemeral discs bearing the songs of a day, as they wander through our parks and along our esplanades with their transistor sets held up like sacred tokens, these kids may

135

seem often to approach a full-time quest for synthetic fun. The Krarls throw fits in the midst of their show that prostrate them on the floor in a writhing mass. Four times they are led off the stage by their henchmen, clothed in black cloaks. And four times they break away from their arms to return to once more scream, screech, howl, gibber, bark back once more into frenzy. This group, their manager says, has had thirty-two hit records in a row. They sell up to a million records each time. The music swells up again, it's not possible to hear the words of the man who's announcing them, the great curtains shift back, and then, of a sudden, there they are, hurtling forward down towards the audience on sleek groovey pads; they are singing already although we can't hear them, bawling, yelling their heart out; Billy Krarl stretches out his arm and grabs the mike as though it were an adversary. His suit is a deep brown mahogany colour, his shirt is a ravishing shade of pink and his boots 'cocoa-butter suede'. He's a lovely piece. Now, of a sudden, he ducks, as if assailed with blows. Sharply, he dances. Sliding, crawling, gyrating, sobbing, and then leaping, barking, searching, screeching he is in gyratory motion as if on rotten casters or carried on the fleecy surface of foam, or staggering on the glassy top of ice. His feet go in all directions, too fast almost to see them, sleek sharp short-circuiting feet, through-putting to ecstasy. Wow, he can dance. And now, faintly audible through the constant screaming we hear actual words:

'Shout! Shout!
Knock yourself out!'

The audience is with them one hundred per cent now, yes, really, one hundred per cent, three hundred per cent, the boys are approaching wildness and the girls are going with them. They're surging down to the stage now, there is a hysterical gasping look in the eyes of the girls, as they go edging down towards the stage, you can't stop them, you can't keep them back. The henchmen have got the boys now, they've put over them those heavy black cloaks, they want to get them away out of here before the fans tear their clothes, but they break from them, they thrust aside the heavy black cowls, they want to return to their fans and give them more, now they are kicking at them with their cocoa-butter suede boots and Billy Krarl is breaking away from them once more, shuddering, gyrating, oh, he's going into another fit, yeah, it's no good, he's down on the floor once more, foaming, the henchmen they are back, they lift the boy up, straighten him out, try desperately to get him back on cue but now he hears the stentorian tones of the pounding organ, he hears it and his nostrils flare like a warhorse, useless their trying to hold him, he is breaking away once more, he wants to give them more and now the whole auditorium is raving and rushing him, there are girls fainting in the aisles girls girls girls and the unutterable yearning scream of thousands of girls in their last stages, the henchmen once more try to get him but now he breaks away, he's back. No, they've got him, they're carrying him out, no, once more he's got free, he's giving them it all now. When Billy Krarl was young he was so poor that his underwear was made from flour sacks.

'I can't get no, Oh, no, no. Hey, hey, hey.
That's what I say. I can't get no, I can't get no,
I CAN'T GET NO SATISFACTION, SATISFAC-
TION, NO SATISFACTION, NO SATISFACTION.'

And now they're in the country. In their thousands they are moving across the land like a swarm of locusts. There is the clatter on tarmac of the boys' high-heeled shoes, and they are approaching through the park of a lovely stately home in the shires. Police cars too are converging on the area. Policemen disguised as teenagers too, with guitars slung over their shoulders. The great eighteenth-century trees hang down over the motley gang. There is the shape of the lovely building ahead, through the foliage.

They bear with them transistor sets tuned to their own wave-born pirate stations, where the disc-jockeys speak so unbelievably fast that you'd think they might be possessed. They're passing through the low-flung branches now of plane trees, gazelles, nudists, bison, aristocrats, leopards and other strange beasts gaze out in wonder from behind the shrubbery at their first sight of teenage man. Now they have reached the stately home, its antique portals protected by vast wooden barricades which, nonetheless, will have all fallen by the end of the day.

They pay now, their thousands of five shillings, but there are many who will not pay, who instead will break through the barriers. And now the mighty hanging loudspeakers belch forth, and another stately ritual is in progress.

'Don't you feel like crying baby, come on, baby, come on, come on, come on, cry, cry, cry, cry, cry . . .'

In the street three girls are standing. One has a rather ill-fitting Victorian dress in brocade. One, with light pink lipstick, is shy, stands against the railings. The third is nondescript. As we go up the steps the first girl says: 'Excuse me, do the Krarls live here?' 'I don't know.' 'They told us they live here.' 'We'll go and ask for you.' We go up to the flat they show us, and bang on the door. An angry woman confronts us and kicks our dog as it tries to run in. 'Do the Krarl Brothers live here?'

'Any more of this and I'll ring the law.'

Of course, the girls must have been ringing the bell. We go out and tell them. 'Oh Lord, and we come all the way from Bumley,' says the plumpest of the girls. 'And we ain't had no breakfast.'

'What makes you think they live here?'

'We met a fella in the street and he told us. We come down without any breakfast to see the Krarl Brothers, and the lorry driver we come with said, They live in Soho. So we went to

Soho and there we met a fella and he told us they live here. We know they live in London. We come down once before and we saw them, they was in a big Rolls. We tried to lie down in front of it but they drove round us.'

Synthetic fun in its purest form issues from the mouths of our disc-jockeys. Some get hooked on this life of concocting in air-conditioned studios their lonely bonhomie. Others get wild to escape. Thousands and thousands of letters pour in to them. As well as from teenagers, they are from women who've got stuck in adolescence.

A disc-jockey: 'I have about 6,000 letters at home, so many I can't get through my front door. Often, I follow them up. I go and call on one of these Mrs Women (they either love being

called that, or hate it). I just drop in for a friendly cup of tea and a bit of a chinwag, and it's great fun. Sometimes their husbands are at home and they are always glad to see me. But I don't think they'd be so pleased if they knew what their wives had written to me in the first place.'

As well as the disc-jockeys, there are the pirate newscasters. Radio London claim that they 'Tell you more, say it better.' One of the newscasters was recently asked where he got the news from. He replied: 'Well, that's a big question. Someone else might get the idea too.'

Martin Fairfax: 'Some of the male groups go sex crazy – this is specially true of the new ones who are just beginning to make it. It goes to their heads. The more established ones often have rather nice and decent girl friends, but the new ones like to play the world. They really do have a new girl friend each night. They get a fantastic sense of unreality, it's surprising that more of them don't go off their rocker. At the opening night of *Maggie May* in the provinces two members of the pop group electrocuted themselves and had to be taken to hospital. It's the same with the whole of their lives. They're plugged in to something so vast it could kill them. They get a fantastic feeling of over-exposure and it's bad for them. This feeling that all they have to do is go to a window and wave their hand and fifty-seven girls will go crazy.'

And this restless music of sex and fulfilment breeds also its casualties. Like the young girls who wander round Britain, lost, longing, trying to recognize landmarks in this land that conforms so little to the land they're really trying to find. Somewhere in the subtopian nightmare their dream is lost.

Later, when the dream fades, girls write to magazines about their boy friends:

'He's very suitable really. He's a proper mod and he's got all the things a mod should have – a scooter, a transistor, boots,

140

etc. etc. Yes, he's ideal. I don't really know why I still have my doubts.'

'Ravers they are, mostly, the ones that go on the island,' says Jim. 'But not all them here are *real* ravers.'

We climb the narrow sixty-foot humped bridge in the darkness, with underneath the blue Thames water sliding. A scarred notice at the farther end says 'Eel Pie Island'.

The tide is high. We have to wade a few steps to get to the bridge. Now the foliage is dark, and rain-drenched laurel slashes across our faces. Amidst the bushes, scuffling. Ahead, seen through the branches, a few little bungalows on stilts and beyond them the 'Hotel', glimmering dimly. Once it was a fashionable rendezvous. Now it's become rave-centre and dreamworld for the youth of the soft Western underbelly of London, haven for students and layabouts, mouldering just upstream from Richmond like something from the American South. Innumerable youths lounge outside on the blue and white cracked diagonal tiles. We push through them, arrive in a hall crammed with ravers, smelling of damp and Guinness, and where the juke-box blares. Three boys guard the entrance. It's hard to talk our way in. Girls are holding out their wrists to be stamped with 'Eelpieland' in phosphorescent letters. We stumble into the room and the stench and mildewy warmth of the place wash over us as if we were in a bath. A juicesome doll is dancing in mid floor with a succession of partners, sometimes collapsing into the arms of some man at the side of the room, then she returns to the floor, dancing amid the thousand odd others.

A rather beautiful lanky-haired girl with a sigh, in a sulky voice: 'Well, it's a way of relaxing, you know, and releasing the pent-up emotions that you collect inside you during the week.'

'The theory is,' says Ray, 'that the girls who come here are more intelligent than the girls at the Palais and the modern jazz clubs. Unfortunately this is becoming increasingly untrue as time goes on because they're all deserting the Palais and the modern clubs and come to do a bit of raving here. But there's still a few left that you can talk to, and until we can find where the really intelligent girls go we'll just have to keep coming here, I suppose.'

'They had some pictures of this place in the Sunday papers,' says Ray: 'It was very sad really. Next day we were besieged, besieged by businessmen. Left their Bentleys on the shore, you know, and their chauffeurs. With neatly furled umbrellas, queueing in the bushes.'

'What were they queueing for?'

'Dunno. Some of the pictures were, you know, luscious. Neckin' in the bushes.'

'Did they get in?'

'Don't suppose so.'

Jim says: 'What helps is its being an island. It helps to think you're going into your own world with your own people surrounding you.'

Jim McDonnell: 'The stars represent the ideal. They live in a continual urging of pop music, surrounded by devices for the enjoyment of leisure, go to clubs, stay up all night, have a superfluity of drink, cars, girl friends. What is being sold is something that's anti-social which is then combined with something else like beauty, clothes, intelligence. What this anti-social thing shows is affluent organized blunk, the only responsibility being personal security, a bed for the night, a girl friend, a joint, a dose of L.S.D. Shout, Shout, Knock Yourself Out! as the song goes. Rock 'n' Roll started all this off. The basic ideal behind it has always been anti-social.'

The following pills could be bought in the park near the Madhouse Hotel: French Blues, Green and Whites, Brown and Whites, Browns, and Black Bombers. Price between 9d. and 2s. 6d. each.

Rave: 'A lot of the attitudes of "The Who" are destructive. They batter their instruments to bits when they are on stage. "It's great," Keith said. "You swipe out at the drum and hear them rip and the kick is fantastic."

'"When I bash my guitar to pieces I feel like I'm tight and floating" says Pete. "The Who" are aware of looks. They would never date a girl who didn't look good.'

'Toots' Camarata: 'Most of the groups are not part of the music business anyway ... they're as near to being in the clothing business as they are to music.'

Norrie Archer: 'The Twist was symbolic of its time. The lower half of the body representing sex and passion, gyrates. But the upper half, the reason, keeps cool.'

Jim McGuinn of The Byrds: 'The noise of the aeroplane in the forties was a rrrooooaaaahhhh sound – so Sinatra and other people sang like that with those sort of overtones. Now we've got the krrrriiiisssshhhh jet sound and the kids are singing up there now. It's the mechanical sounds of the era; the sounds are different and the music is different. It also has the following ingredients: Latin and blues and jazz flavours, Anglo-Saxon church music, Negro music.'

> 'Here it comes
> Here it comes
> Here it comes
> Here it comes
> Here comes your nineteenth nervous breakdown'

A three-year-old boy went into a newsagent and asked for a grave for his sister. No one could understand what he was talking about, until the newsagent was able to identify what he wanted as a copy of *Rave* magazine.

And Dusty is part of this scene, Dusty, the girl they call the 'moodiest, goodliest, girl on the scene ... a sparkling package.' Dusty finds 'twirling things around' one way of relieving tension. She has a 'honeyed, husky voice' which makes for 'great singing'.

An ad in *Boyfriend:*

Music is essential for love. We don't reckon you can lose your heart without it. Think – how else could you dance (smoochy creep, if you prefer), give parties, attract boys on the beach, or be tuned into the boys who are singing about love?

Those who doubt the strength of the religion of rave should visit somewhere like Kirkwall in the Orkneys. There, looking across the island to the grey sea, and the rounded island of Hoy, they may see the frilly girls in the very latest gear, listening to the juke-box, dancing to the music, the lingua franca of our time, as it streams out across the cold Arctic Ocean...

A pop singer: 'We went to play in this prison and the fella next to me took one gulp of tea and then he spat it out. You see, it had got bromide in it. But me I'd drunk two cups already and when I got back to my wife that night she was very sexy and I just couldn't make it with her. It was all very sad. Then we discovered that others of the pop groups were having the same trouble. They just couldn't make it at all. And they were losing all their ability and all their fans, all the ones who had played in prisons, it was drinking this prison tea what did it, they couldn't sing their music right any more so that was the start of the rot.'

Jet Harris, ex of the Shadows, claimed in the *People:* 'Big Beat? Dead Beat! Yes, that's me . . . all of a sudden my nerves couldn't stand the rat race. The pace . . . the forty-eight hours' work crammed into each twenty-four hours . . . the through-the-night travelling to one-night stands . . . the noise of the fans . . . yes, screaming, shouting, hair-tugging fans . . . I collapsed in a bundle of nerves. The jet had burned itself out . . .'

The present scene began when Bill Haley and his Comets came over to Britain. It was these men that introduced in

144

Rock'n'Roll the type of wild, dynamic, demoniac blunk music that is still with us. They were the pioneers and in their music and themselves they were rough. Climax of their show was when the saxophonist hurled himself down on his back on the floor and waved his legs around, pounding them on the boards. The others nodded their heads at each other (amidst the pervading din) as if to say 'He's well away.' And then, what's this, oh, it's the bass player and he's laid his bass on its side on the floor and he's plucking away at it wildly and now he's jumped upon it so that he straddles it, legs either side in a most pornographic position. These rough diamonds went back to the States. But there were new faces to come, new faces.

The *Elvis Monthly* ('Always 100% Elvis') reveals that he is still top of the pops, once again perched on the top as both the 'World Male Singer' and also 'World Musical Personality'. *Elvis Monthly* is published from 'Elvisville' at 41 Derby Road, Heanor, Derbyshire. It includes a weekly feature called 'Who's What in Elvisville', and another called 'Here, There, and Elviswhere'. There is also a compendium of facts about Elvis called, of course, 'Elcyclopedia'. One of the more moving items is a weekly column entitled 'Discovering Elvis' in which a different girl tells how she first became a fan: 'Well, there was I, a girl of eleven years old who previously hadn't known what a pop singer was, suddenly thrust into the crazy world of an El-fan!

'I bought every Elvis mag that I could lay my hands on, every record I could afford and saw every movie as many times as my parents would let me (sometimes more!) and I was so-o-o-o-o HAPPY!

'Because I stuck to Elvis through thick and thin, cried for him, laughed for him, and prayed for him and acted like a typical El-fan!

'My greatest moment came on Tuesday the 7th of April 1966. This is what I wrote in my diary on that day: "At 8.45

a.m. Mum came in with a letter. She gave it to me, it had El's name and address in the top left hand corner and it was postmarked MEMPHIS!!!! I opened it with trembling hands and it was the most beautiful Easter card. I burst into tears and sat on my bed shivering and sobbing on Mum's shoulder for the next five minutes. I have never cried so much with happiness in my entire life!"'

There is also a *Rolling Stones Book* and *Beatle Book*. Signing herself 'Luv, a Beatle Person who loves you very, very much,' Lynn Rubin writes: 'Because you were "cooped-up" in your rooms on the 18th floor of the Sheraton-Lincoln Hotel, you didn't see what was happening on the ground below. Girls, a few blocks away from the hotel, were screaming for no apparent reason!'

Another girl, writing to *Rave*, mentions in a letter mainly about something else, how she and a friend managed to 'break down a door' and get into the Stones' dressing-room.

Another girl: 'What more can my friend and I do to meet the Stones? About eight weeks ago we ran away from home to meet them. We thumbed up to London on a Wednesday night, and arrived at one in the morning. We walked around all night. Thursday daytime we walked around London, trying to find the Stones, but didn't succeed. That night we slept in a park. The third day we went to the Marquee club in Wardour Street and met the Boz People. But that night the police picked us up and that was the end of our Stones hunt. We spent the night in prison and our parents came to get us out at two-thirty the next day.'

Rave runs a Missing Column which they call 'Boys and Girls Lost and Found.'

A girl: 'We would like to get in touch with some boys who were in Bournemouth at the end of July. We don't know their names but one of them had a red waistcoat and long dark hair. They had a blue Hillman, number 4650 KV.'

A girl: 'In July I met a boy called Rob Saunders. He told me he came from Cannington Young Farmers Institute, and lived near Wells, although he really came from London. He is tall, dark haired, eighteen, and is a Rocker. Please find him because I want to see him again.'

A girl: 'In August we met Chris who lives in Lowestoft and Roger who lives in Bath. We met them while camping at Lowestoft. They are both about seventeen–eighteen with blond hair. Chris has a scooter with number plates 320 VCF. Please tell them to write. We miss them dearly.'

A girl: 'The girls that go to the big London beat dance halls are the sort that, you know, don't want regular boy friends, they may think they do but the pull and the glamour of these places is too strong for them. And they live, a lot of them, by shoplifting. They go out to Bromley, Ilford, pay a driver to go, whip a few clothes, then they come back to Soho. And often the sort of men there are the ones that threaten. They say, Unless you come up and have one in the office upstairs, your face'll get razor slashes over it. Then there won't be even nobody *wants* to have it.

'Or they take you out for a coffee in their car, and they give you what they say are aspirins. But they're not, you never get there.'

'The Krarls' road manager embezzled them out of thousands of pounds. Their car broke down and they rang him and asked for a fiver but he wouldn't help.'

A girl: 'I'm the secretary for the Krarl fan club actually, I get the strangest letters – "Your dress is disgusting, I saw you with Tony Krarl and you're not fit to wipe his bottom." The typical sort of letter the boys get goes: "I saw you in Brixton the other day, I wonder did you see me? I was the third girl on the corner and I was wearing a pink two-piece." So then I have to write back as if it was the boys. "Yes, of course I saw you, I remember most clearly, you were the attractive one."'

147

'The Krarls used to hang round their flat till a bird turned up. They kidnapped a girl once for a week. She lived in their flat and did all the washing-up for them and washed all their clothes. Then they threw her out.

'Some girls are gone on pop stars, they hang around waiting for whichever celebrity's down that week, round the local dance hall, so they can have him.'

Another girl tells me: 'I saw you talking to the secretary of the Krarls' fan club. Well, she blackmails them into sleeping with her. The thing is she's the only one who knows Billy Krarl's real age, and that he wears a toupee, and that he's married. And she edits *Grunt*, so she's always threatening to expose him, so then he has to sleep with her.'

'Once I met some fella, he was a road manager he was, he said the Beatles were really fairly elderly men, they were one of those concert party groups in the Nineteen Twenties, and they did a come-back, now in wigs and chest-wigs and corsets . . .'

'Don't you feel like crying, come on baby, come on, come on, come on, cry, cry, cry, cry . . .'

The girl that wants to be a pop singer enters the coffee bar, squashes down past the coffee machine, past the pictures of Screaming Lord Sutch, past tiny girlies with bright eyes. Past the belting moronic scream of the quivering juke-box, past lonely sailors in their sleazy civvy suits, down the narrow length of the bar while the box shouts, fortissimo:

> 'Some day they'll see
> That from the start
> My place has been
> Deep in your heart'

She passes more bold-faced girlies with mascara-bordered eyes and pays out three bob to go downstairs, down a steep staircase where a different beat can be heard; throbs more plush and insistent even than the thump of the jukebox. She gets to the bottom, the room is packed with kids twisting, kids standing around in the darkness. They shake together girl with girl, and the boys in sharp suits and with-it hair-styles stand in groups round the walls in darkness, and at one end a band, four boys belting out the Blue Beat with such verve that you'd think the devil was in them.

From a door at the back the proprietor emerges. He is a short man in a seedy suit. He leads her back with him into a brightly lit yellow-walled room piled high with hamburger cartons and other rubbish.

He turns to her: 'I believe that you may be in on the start of one of the biggest things to come out of this century. Show me how you move. I want you to do the shake.'

Obediently, the girl shakes a little, waving her arms and legs.

'Yes, I discovered them all. Been going seven years now and I'm still making discoveries. I'm quite a dynamic fellow. If I get results I'm happy, but if I don't I start pushing and shoving till I do. I can do something for you.

'I used to be a stunt-man actually. Riding, swimming, falling off buildings, you know. Which gets me back to you, Darlene. Yes, I've been in this business seven years, and I'm still making discoveries. Billy Krarl, Rock Clifford, Ron Amuk, Furious Blackett, the Earl of Why ... you name him, I found him ... and in the future names as big ... *bigger*.

'Which gets me back to you.

'When you first came here to the cellar, you never dreamed of being a star, did you, you were just a London student. I then observed that you was very smart, very popular with the boys here, and attractive. I asked you if you had ever considered taking up showbiz. At that time you was only a student but later, one year later, you came back and asked me was I serious in what I'd said. I said I was.'

'And now –' Darlene says.

'And now you're topping the bill at Southall next week.'

A coin telephone rings beside him. He speaks: 'Yes, well it's like any other package show. A girl and a boy and a boy and a girl, and a trumpet. And like every dance-hall, they'll want a little of the sweet stuff. All right?'

The girl: 'If you've not made it before you're twenty-one, you're never going to make it in this game. I had a boy friend. We used to go for walks, go to the pictures. All that stuff. Then this came up. Now, I wonder whatever I was thinking of.'

The proprietor: 'You're going to be big. I can always tell. I'm not a musical man myself but I can hear the beat through the wall. I can hear what they like. I know that you will be big. As big as any so far. *Bigger*.'

Outside, back in the shake cellar, a girl in jeans and with chunky dirty sweater is twisting, and the boy behind the microphone on the stage is pulling it back towards him, yelling:

'And I like it
    Always hearing ya say
  Yer liking it too.'

The girl's Lone Ranger jeans are tight round her haunches. A boy says: 'She's on to a good thing mate. They all started here. Ron Amuk, Rock Clifford.'

'No more. There's money after these boys now. When he had them playing here at a pound a head a night, it was because the big money wasn't involved yet. He don't make it no more.'

'She's going to make it.'

'I don't think.'

The girl in rough unkempt hairy sweater and Lone Ranger jeans: 'I'm fed up with all this new stuff. It's like the whole thing has disintegrated. The dances change so fast. Already the Twist's out of date and the Shake. It's as if it's all going faster and faster, the whole world's breaking down. You get a whole room doing a new one like "Radioactive", you think they've all gone off their heads.'

A boy: 'Not like when you were fourteen.'

A boy: 'Try the bluebeat, dear. Start on the Blues, and then wave . . . all the squares good-bye.'

'She can't sing anyway.'

A boy: 'She can move.'

The girl says: 'It's all going. The mods are having it all their own way now. They've won their last battle. The Rocker is replaced by the Neatnik. It was the Beatles that started it,

when the Beatles put on suits. It used to be mods that dressed up and Bohemians that didn't. But now there's no place for the Bohemians.'

A boy: 'People that keep up with fads must be ready for anything.'

The girl: 'There's less and less of my friends now, every day I find that one of them has cut their hair or settled for a job. It's the pressure of everyone against them. One of them gets inside, and when he comes out, he's a different person, he jumps, he conforms, he jumps whenever he sees the law.'

A few weeks later Darlene's picture is in all the papers – but not exactly in the circumstances that her manager imagined.

It turns out that she's become engaged to a sheikh. And as a result of that it also transpires that Darlene has never been a little girl – only a big one.

Two years before she changed from a boy to a girl.

'We live near one of the theatres where the Krarls went when they were on tour, and there's these kids camped outside for two or three days before they come down from the North and they settle down there on the pavement and all through the night and you can hear them chanting, "We want the Krarls, we want the Krarls" although the Krarls are miles away. And we went in, we felt we had to, we felt that this was one thing we couldn't miss ever, and we were standing there, and it was incredible, the noise of screaming was so loud you couldn't hear the Krarls at all, it was painful on the eardrums. And all around us there were girls, some of them eleven and twelve, like, I think this was being their first sexual experience, their faces were twisted in a sort of agony, they seemed really sent to the point. They just couldn't stop screaming. I felt amazed that humans could be like that, and amazed that I might be like that because I'm human too. My sister's like that. She was sitting the other night and watching the Telly, and then Billy

152

Krarl came on and she screamed. She literally screamed. She was just sitting in our living-room and suddenly she screamed!

'And she was always especially sent by P. J. Proby, so one day a friend rang up and he said, P. J. Proby wants to meet her. I've told him about her and he's most enthusiastic, he wants to meet her. So I rang her up and I said, "Guess what, P. J. Proby wants to meet you!" And she said, "Oh how fabulous! I'll be along!" But a little bit later she rang up and said: "I don't think I can" and I said "Why ever not?" and she said "I can't go through with it. I just wouldn't be able to control myself." I said, "Don't be ridiculous. Anyway, that's probably precisely what he wants." But she said, "No, I'm sorry. I really can't. I just wouldn't be able to control myself if I met him. I would scream." She's got two kids by the way. She needs a man. And since then she hasn't had no boy friend.

'We went on tour and then one night we were in the same digs as the Higgins Sisters – you know what that's like – well, they're famous for it, boys boys boys, it's in out in out all night. And underneath us there was this American singer, and he went for my sister, and he had her and then he broke her heart.'

And from among the crowds that line the street a young man emerges, dancing on his suede soles, dodging among the crowd on the pavement. Dodging back. He halts. Spins round. He speaks, urgently but incomprehensibly, in a fast burr. A farmer's boy, you might think, there's a rustic openness about him, a feeling still of straw adhering to his luxuriantly waving hair. He dances about as he talks to you, in a crazy cascade that is quite incomprehensible. Suddenly he starts back, dances into an alley, beckoning. You follow. Above the alley a notice says: 'True Love Social Club.' But there's nothing but rubbish in the alley. The panelled Georgian houses stretch up overhead, derelict and empty. Nothing but the smell of damp and excrement. He's peeing against a wall.

A street lamp lights his face. You look at him again, note the hectic brilliance of his eyes behind their dark rings, and his lips, purple rimmed as if he had been crushing blackcurrants, breaking out here and there with white pus in their crevices. 'On! Come on! On!' Protective, curious, you follow him along the street. Suddenly he dives down some cellar steps, and pushes open a battered door, many times repaired with different pieces of hardboard. On it, a notice saying *The Palm Beach*. A curious crowd of people down here, sitting around in a series of catacombs, drinking tea. Misshapen women, apparently in finery of the thirties. A little gnome-like man making notes on a pad in the corner.

The vast console of the juke-box lights the young man's face purple as he pushes by among the tables.

'You seen my mate?'

'What mate?'

'What's he talkin' about?'

'You're not in the place you think you are, mate.'

He emerges.

He seizes your lapel in a paroxysm of worry: 'You got your identification on you? Oh, we got to have our identification. Otherwise they can pull you in. Yes, we must have identification. I say I live with you? Say I'm your mate? Address? What address? What address you come from?' He tries to memorize it, but each time it slips from his mind.

Then he seems to recognize something: 'Cobble stones! Coffee Bar! Quick! Find it now!'

He dances off into the street.

Down another staircase. Urgently he peers over the top of a battered door: 'S'il vous plaît? S'il vous plaît?'

But the proprietor, knowing perhaps that he's reached the stage where he's so seedy now that soon he'll be picked up, says: 'It's not this one man, not this one.'

When he emerges to street level again it's as if he's lost some of his grip. He says 'Juke-box. Third traffic lights. Then left. Then cobbles.'

After five minutes' brisk walking his hectic eyes widen slightly with terror. He clutches your arm: 'Fuzz. Keep straight ahead. Keep walking.' Then a little later: 'Cobbles! We're laughing!' Then he dives down a back alley. Then he returns. 'Not there. No more. You been talking. Talking too much. Confused me.'

Five minutes' more brisk walking. He says: 'Traffic lights. Nearly there.' Then more confused gabbling. Then, as if in the grip of some sinister dream, you can understand his words again: 'I . . . Held me down . . . Got the ropes round . . . so I . . . Then the three on them . . . Afore they comes back again . . . Terrible thing . . . And then my mate . . . Good mate . . . Kip up gether . . . That upset me . . . You could take is place, if yer wanta. I said You could take is place if yer wanta. Yer wanta? Kip up with me? Be a place. Good place. You like to be my mate? Goo mate.

'Yeah, gea place there. Snice. Goo places theah.'

But before you can answer, he has forgotten.

'How much you got? Nough for how many? Need sixty a day. Maximum. Three bob each. Pound a week.'

Then later: 'It's tablets for me. But also, we got to drink down tea. But I don't like tea.'

You say: 'Where are you sleeping? What will you do to-night? What do you do ever? You must get off the streets. Someone will get you.'

He says: 'Won't get me. I see them. See'm coming. Anyway, I say, life's short. Got ter live. *Cobble stones! We're home and dry!*'

But we're not.

He turns accusingly at you:

'I was following *you*. I thought *you* knew where we was going. You been talking too much.

'Hey. If we see a juke-box now, that means we been going round in a circle!'

Later: 'I see green.'

'Green. See that green in the middle of the road. That means we've come too far. We're out of London! Into the country!'

He stops someone in the street.

'You seen a coffee bar?'

'Well, there's the Eldorado just over there,' says the perplexed stranger.

'Yes, that's the one, that'sa one we want!'

'But it's closed now.'

He begins to stumble in the wrong direction.

And you say: 'I'm going now.'

And he says: 'See you in one hour. Can really findem. See you by coffee bar just round the corner from where I met you. Like this.'

He demonstrates the corner with his arm. He staggers, loses his balance.

Good-bye. Good-bye.

He's gone. But he's got money. You gave him money. He's got money. Life-buying money.

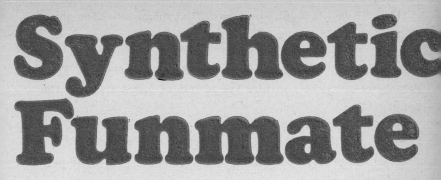

Synthetic Funmate

What sort of person ought you to be to qualify as a synthetic fun person? At this point we can perhaps begin to get a picture of the ideal synthetic fun *mate*. And let it be said at once, albeit with regret, that as things are at the moment, and speaking for the time being mainly of physical matters, it is somewhat easier for a girl to achieve this synthetic state than it is for a man.

True, there are things that a man can do. He can pad his shoulders, or jack himself up on special shoes whose heels contain 'concealed inches'.

He can wear corsets, or rubber reduction garments. Or sew into his trousers an artificial penis. ('We're dressing in the middle, man,' a pop singer recently was quoted as claiming.) His face may be given a more artificial mould with a variety of face creams, conditioners, moisturizers, and eye pads. He may garnish himself in masculine shades like Healthy Tan and Outdoor Bronze, or drench his body in a perfume called Aramis, companion to the feminine scent 'Youthdew'. ('It's a very manly odour, not sweet at all, but if he likes Youthdew on her then she'll like Aramis on him.') He may use a face mask to smooth away lines, or a friction lotion. A 'face powder in three shades', a 'pickup mask', a 'lip pomade' and a hair spray may also form part of his equipment. He can labour to acquire 'a wonderful golden tan . . . without the sun'. He can deck himself out in a large and growing variety of synthetic lotions and scents. Synthetic teeth, false eyes, artificial limbs of various types and designs may be of help. He may wear a wig or chest wig or dye his hair. He may build up his body to an acceptable size with the aid of body-building courses, chest-expanders, stationary tricycles, dumb-bells, chin bars, etc.

But alas, here the list stops.

For women, I am glad to say, much more can be done in the way of synthetic embellishment. Indeed, structural alterations may be undertaken. 'God's chosen sex' can come to seem not unlike that picture of Dali's in which a woman's gangrenous thighs and breasts are supported on a series of props and crutches. Only from in front does all seem genuine, sound, and self-supporting.

The methods available for changing the human female are really extremely profuse. Not only her physical state but also her personality may be tinkered with. The following adjuncts, limbs and traits may be obtained changed or adapted synthetically: hair, voice, complexion, jaw, ears, nose, eyes, eyelashes, arms, legs, bosom, feet, buttocks, midriff, smiles, laughs, method of sitting down, climbing stairs, walking, skin, freckles, thighs, and other areas. Attitudes and behaviour to other people are also important and should follow the accepted pattern.

Let's start at the top, with synthetic *hair*. It should be piled in mountains into the sky, and be, ideally, entirely artificial. As the *Observer* puts it: 'Girls have become highly ingenious at developing the use of hairpieces, top-knots, wigs, and switches, giving a large variety of styles and changes of personality.' Note the idea of a change of personality here. Methods of producing a new synthetic personality are especially to be valued.

A change in your hair *colour* may also work wonders. A Mayfair hairdresser writes: 'If you're tired of being you and

158

subscribe to the theory that blondes *do* have more fun – then have it with your hair tinted Blonde Beige or Gazelle (Rumour has it that you're right!)'

A young night-club singer who always wore wigs was wondering how to attract attention to herself when she arrived at London Airport. Her personal agent hit on an idea. As she got off the plane she was waving a gorgeous auburn wig. And the head of this attractive girl was completely shaved bare.

From the hair we now pass to what lies below it – the synthetic face. A good deal of trouble should be taken here. Indeed, trouble *is* taken. Thanks to an 'aggressive sales policy' standardized faces are even spreading as far as the Outer Isles. Mr Lowe, a London businessman, recently hired a statistician to find out how many work hours his female staff were using to put on make-up and generally tart themselves up. The statistician estimated that, between the ages of fifteen and seventy-five, the average British woman spends four years and fourteen weeks in this occupation. A fashion magazine – *Vogue* – reminds us: 'Skin that looks natural is a different story from wearing no make-up.' As illustration of this statement it shows a radiant healthy-looking country girl, wisps of straightish hair blending well with a piece of straw that she holds in her hand. Shortly, no doubt, she will be putting it in her mouth. Clearly she must be in the country. And what a picture of natural health, you might think. But no. Here is how it was achieved:

A skin, pale by nature, subtly warmed with Lancôme's Souple Foundation in the shade called Brise, Sable powder, and Moderato rouge. Eyes again are made up to look natural – lashes darkened with Noir mascara, lids lightened with the silvery shade of Ombre Mat Shadow called Gris . . .

Another magazine has mentioned that 'every woman' should spend at least a pound a week on her face. If by any chance, in achieving this synthetically natural look you are plagued by rather too natural a character written by time into your face, it is time to experiment with another useful synthetic device – the so-called 'Cinderella' ointment which, applied before a 'date', it is claimed, entirely banishes all those tell-tale boring marks of your own personality, such as wrinkles, puffs under the eyes, 'laugh lines', etc. but only for a while. Five hours or so later, like evening dew, your own face creeps back again.

Of course, not only the skin of your face, but what lies underneath it is also important, namely, your *personality*. This should be sought with almost as much care as a passable face or body. And one word of advice here: Do not be afraid. Do not fear to reject your real self and thus leave a space for the more acceptable synthetic self that will come in its place.

The first thing is to discover what sort of 'type' you are. In one academy that teaches such things 'the beginner is advised what basic type she is.' She then 'learns what is acceptable as to smiles and expressions . . .' and also 'acquires a number of basic poses suitable for her type.'

As well as smiles and expressions, the *method of speaking* should also be studied. 'If your English has been holding you back,' says the Concert Hall Record Club, 'if faulty diction, incorrect grammar, colourless voice or regional speech habits are robbing you of social and financial success . . . here is a proven new method.' Under a photograph of two distinguished persons looking at a brash and self-confident young man with distinct hostility as if he had a form of verbal B.O., they write that they can teach you to speak the words of the English language 'as they are spoken by persons of breeding and accomplishment'. They go on to speak of the great verbal artists who 'make of their voices a rich and varied adventure in listening . . . Friends can't tell you and your business associates won't . . . what hampering speech mannerisms may be

160

interfering with your social and financial success.' What they call speech 'grooming' can, they mention, mean 'the difference between merely being alive and really living'.

Not only how you say it but also *what you say* may be important. A magazine gives the following tips: 'Develop a liking for music, arts, current events, etc. . . . A keen interest in these will sharpen your mind and furnish you with a vast reservoir of good topics for conversation . . . too often lack of something to talk about has ruined many a prospective romance . . .'

Instructions for the further standardization of the human creature are given in books by the organizer of a model school – Mary Young. One book contains a 'before and after' picture showing the change of an attractive girl into something more synthetic. The author comments: 'I have observed again and again the transformation that takes place.' Girls, she says, should make out a list of their good and bad points. Good points: budget minded: a general overall neatness. Bad points: a 'scatty' look: a too solemn or serious look. Next: facial expression and posture. The sort of thing to watch here is, when in a strong wind don't let the expression on your face say 'I just can't bear it.' Instead 'try relaxing your face to the wind, thinking "wonderful cold wind", and pretending that you are thoroughly enjoying it.' Watch your face too when walking. Let some piece of music run through your head. By doing this you will 'walk through the street to the strain of some glorious music singing in your mind. (But only in quiet streets, please, not where there is traffic.)'

If all these devices fail to get the correct look into your face and eyes it may be time to consider actual structural alterations. These should be achieved with help from the new craft of Face Lifting. A Beautician should make incisions at your temples and behind your ears. Your facial skin should be then gently detached from its underlying tissue, and the surplus skin which has stretched into wrinkles gently eased and smoothed outwards – 'like smoothing a counterpane'.

If you're worried that it may hurt or take up a lot of time, the following may reassure you: a reshaped nose leaves no scars since the operation is done inside the nose, but it will be bruised and a little swollen for a couple of weeks and may be accompanied by one or two black eyes.

Eyes: These should be synthetically stained with eye make-up, or rounded and made mysteriously convex with contact lenses. An extension of this is 'pop-eyes' – that device whereby eyes can be made striped like a unicorn, fringed with petals, feathers or hearts. Such synthetic eyes should be fringed with synthetic *lashes*: these range from very fine, real hair lashes, 'ideal for day wear', to 'dark, devastating fur and fabulous "sable-style" for evening wear' ... one, especially to be recommended, has 'rich, double density that combines the softness of Natural Fur with the strength and finish of Real Hair.' The eyelashes themselves may also be made longer with an interesting product, namely 'Eyelash Grower'. Mrs M.C. of London writes: 'My eyelashes are now just like a filmstar's.'

A diagram which claims to simplify making up the eyes calls for four shades of eye shadow, eyeliner, a sable brush to apply pearly sheen with, eyelashes and tweezers to put them on, a pencil for shaping eyebrows and a brush to smooth them out.

And so we pass to the synthetic *nose*. A too small or stubby nose should be remedied by cutting it open and filling it with slivers of cartilage taken from the hip. A too large nose may be reduced by the same process in reverse – small slivers are taken out, although these need not be re-inserted in the hip. This operation is not painful, although women who have experienced it under local anaesthetic sometimes say that they found the sound of sawing rather peculiar.

Jaws: These may be altered in the same way as noses.

Ears: The lobes may be removed. Or they may be thrust back till they are close to the head.

Teeth: False teeth and or filed teeth may be used.

Lips: Should be painted with lipstick which should not necessarily follow the line of the actual lips. They should be used for *kissing* and a useful work now on the market explains the best way to do this: 'Kiss and cry no more. Your "sexcess" depends on when, how, how much, with whom – and a lot more. It calls for the *right line* and the *sure touch*. Get straightened out and "cued up" . . .'

A more romantic attitude to the kiss is taken in the following description of what it feels like to be touched by the lips of Elvis: 'A kiss is not given by Elvis lightly. Elvis does not believe in kissing every girl that he comes across. Girls who have been kissed by Elvis treasure the feel of his lips in their hearts for they know that it is remembered also in a corner of Elvis' heart.'

Gums: should be coloured with cosmetic toothpaste. Gordon Moores is a good one: it 'shines your teeth as bright as fashion jewels, tints up your gums to please the men once more and yet again – poor fools.'

And so we pass down from the head to the ideal *synthetic body*. For now bodies no less than faces should be packaged and standardized. There is a body of the year just as there is a face of the year. A magazine mentions that the key points for this year are: 'litheness of leg, a slim young-swimmer look to the shoulders, a flat young look to the waist and midriff . . .'

One way of achieving this, it explains, is with 'Firm Second Skin: flesh-coloured wisps of firm second skin which make the body look controlled but lithe . . .' As a result of these wisps, so the magazine further reveals: 'The adaptability of girls for reshaping is indubitable: when bosoms and soft shoulders are in, that's what we see. When wasp waists are the thing, girls' middles grow miraculously little.'

Corsets are also a useful addition in this area. Speaking of the waist, Wallace Sharps, president of the Society of Beauticians, explains that, until recently, only older women used corsets. 'The corset manufacturers suddenly woke up to this fact and changed the whole nature of their industry and multiplied their sales in a fantastic way. They did this by putting over the simple statements that every fashion needs a particular shape and also that no woman can rely on looking perfect without some form of figure control.'

The texture of the body as well as its shape should be watched carefully. *Synthetic smoothness* may be obtained with the Electrolysis system. An electric current is transmitted to the base of the hair, through a needle, thus killing it. But this method is painful and only fairly intrepid females have so far made use of it. If electrolysis scares you, then you should try Short Wave Diathermy. One hair every fifteen seconds can be removed by this method, which also depends on a needle and an electric current, but is less painful. Waxing is yet another, rather more primitive method. Hot wax is laid over the body. It cools and hardens, encasing the hair. Then wax and hair together are wrenched off. As it does not destroy the hair at the follicle, waxing only lasts until the next growth of hair has arrived. It will thus have to be done fairly frequently. An expert comments: 'From a beautician's point of view this in itself is not such a bad idea, as it provides regular treatment possibilities.' Skin may also be burned off, thus revealing the soft under-skin that lies beneath it.

Legs and arms, if not of standard size, should be operated on to make them more so. Girls have recently been operated on to cut as much as six inches off both arms and legs.

As well as vertical extra inches, the ideal synthetic person should also keep an eye on their *horizontal inches*. Rubber reducing garments may be useful here with which to sweat it out. Suntex Rubber Slimwear comes in black, white,

'CHEMMY'

This mad little number in patent night-blue rubberised peau de soie tops off your kinky boots.

Price 69/11 middle-weight rubber.

89/11 swelter-weight rubber.

DRESS

Be a cocktail sensation. Lose weight between 6 and 8. Send body measurements including inside arm.

Price 69/11 middleweight rubber.

89/11 swelter-weight rubber.

PANTALOON SUIT

Zip into a model-girl contour and shed that surplus in silky-smooth rubber. Send body measurements including shoulder to crutch.

Price 79/11 middle-weight rubber.

99/11 swelter-weight rubber.

NIGHT DRESS

Low lights — bedtime reduction. When it's time for bed, **slip** into these rubber frills.

Price 69/11 middle-weight rubber.

99/11 swelter-weight rubber.

semi-transparent, red, yellow, and powder blue rubber. In the words of an advertisement: 'Lose ugly fat you hate . . .' Natural beauty, natural limbs, natural complexion are *not* enough. They *must* be reinforced by artificial means. The hairdresser Alan Spiers mentions: 'Beauty needs genius. And Genius *is* Alan Spiers.'

Spiers explains: 'You might feel that beauty can stand alone; that beauty needs no-one and nothing for its perfection. Well – you'd be wrong!' He explains that in Britain today

Beauty needs genius to keep forever young, to keep ahead of the different facets of fashion which flicker and die. Beauty needs the genius of Alan Spiers. And if you are one of those whose beauty is not instantly self-evident, whose fascination lies more in personality, a quick-silver mind, or grace of movement; then you need the genius of Spiers even more . . . Every woman is beautiful in her own unique way, but it needs the genius of Alan Spiers to project this beauty in a way that is remembered . . .

There are now a whole host of advisers and guides of one sort or another available to replace your old body with a brand-new synthetic one. Mary Young writes: 'Do your *arms* hang tent-wise from your shoulders with your hands looking lost saying "we never know what to do with ourselves"?' If you have this trouble, 'Simply adopt *one* or *two* (but deliberately thrown away, not posed) gestures – hands clasped lightly in front of you, one hand lightly in a pocket, exquisite holding of handbag, one hand delicately touching a fold of a full-skirted dress, etc, etc.'

Most Glorious Attraction

And so, in our tour of the ideal synthetic woman, we reach what is described as 'woman's most glorious attraction.'

And in this area, just as men should be in another, it is desirable that the girls should be jacked up. Their breasts must be raised towards the sky. 'Magic Curve' bras, for instance, 'with built-up cups to give you the voluptuous bustline you have always admired.' Or 'Magic Curve Decollete', described as 'America's latest half-cup bra. Gently lifts the bust giving fuller appearance and extra cleavage.' Breasts must follow the fashion. They must go up, down, out, in, point inwards or outwards, have wide cleavage or no cleavage, according to what's right for the year. One expert tips: 'Imagine that your chest is attached to a pulley in the ceiling while your feet are firmly fixed to the floor and the pulley is gently but firmly stretching you up.'

Sometimes means other than the jack or the hoist may be brought into play.

Butibust, of Brighton, claim:

The soft, enticing contours of a fully-developed feminine bust have persisted throughout the centuries as womanhood's most glorious attraction ... How many deserted wives have said 'What *could* he have seen in her? She has nothing but her figure!' How many girls with little pretensions to beauty, but with gloriously moulded figures, have walked radiantly to the altar with their attractive-faced but bodily undeveloped friends as puzzled and disappointed bridesmaids?

The Butibust treatment consists of rubbing in a cream, and 'scientific manipulation instructions.'

A confidential yet cordial approach is used by the 'Beauty Director' of a Finchley Road, London, product called *Fulbloom*. He writes:

Pull Up a Chair ... and Lets Talk About Fulbloom ... I wish I could welcome you personally ... right here in my office ... where I could tell you about Fulbloom and encourage you in the important work you are about to begin. However, because I am limited to the printed word, I want to extend to you the warmest of welcomes ... even though we cannot meet. I want you to feel that you are seated in my private office and that we are having a heart-to-heart chat. Down through the ages the human female bosom has exercised a most powerful influence over man's philosophies. It has been extolled in religion, literature and folklore ... it has been celebrated in art and song and poetry.

Kurvon of Liverpool is another product with rather similar claims. Although it increases the size of your bosom, Kurvon say that it does not increase your weight. 'The thrilling and exciting secret is that Kurvon contains a valuable and scarce ingredient called Galega – a plant found in the French Mediterranean regions ...'

Pro-Forma, also of Liverpool, write: 'A beautiful bust is every woman's birthright, a feature she is entitled to by being born a woman. But Nature isn't always fair ...' What is the answer? Well, 'British, American and French medical advisers have proved, as a result of their researches and experience, that 'Pro-Forma' ...'

Jane Scott, from a London address, makes a similar point:

A woman's proud possession. A beautiful bosom has always been a source of joy and pride of possession right through the ages. In almost every Art collection. . . . How often has a poor bust brought distress when everything pointed to happiness. *It no longer need be. It is now not unavoidable.*

Jane Scott goes on to point out that her 'pleasant non-greasy cream' can provide 'just the right amount of the feminine glandular ingredient ...'

Jane Scott's follow-up letter, which she sends out to those who don't respond to her pamphlet, is even more eloquent:

The fact that you wrote to me led me to believe you needed assistance, and I am anxious that you start the Treatment without delay and achieve those lovely breasts every woman longs for ...

You well know that a full bosomed feminine figure is one of the Treasures of Life, a source of pride to yourself and a joy to those nearest to you. It is worth a little effort to obtain. So many times the opportunities which come along, things which could change

168

your whole life for the better are just left and not taken.' DONT LET THIS BE ONE OF THEM, do not 'put it off for another day'. Make this a 'day to remember'. Start now with the wonderful Jane Scott Treatment, think what it could do to you . . .

I *really do* look forward to hearing from you, NOW.

Yours sincerely

JANE SCOTT

The order form that accompanies this letter says: 'You will look back on this day with gladness.'

There are many other forms of synthetic breast sweller. The breasts can be cut open and stuffed with yielding plastic, or injected with substance that makes them swell up – sometimes not for ever. The day is surely not far ahead when even nonagenarians will have vast swelling bosoms. Other new methods include injecting the breasts with wax, or grafting in fat tissue. A pad of resistant material may be inserted, but the danger of this is that it may grow hard so that, although it looks right, it may not feel right.

Silicone is probably the best of all ways so far devised. A bag made of silicone membrane and containing silicone in a jelly-like form is inserted in the breasts.

There are also more energetic methods of swelling. Day and night in their homes innumerable women are now at work with 'Venus'. The Venus method involves a rubber bulb which squirts water on to the breasts 'as cold as you can conceivably stand it without shocking the body . . . This treatment sets up a profound stimulation of the blood circulation.' A less ruthless method is a process called 'Aqua-massage – a couple of minutes each day of gentle water massage.' Also much to be recommended is *Aro-Lady*, a battery-driven electric brassiere which surrounds each breast with 'vibratory action'. Booth Elliott & Co. Ltd., who market it, write: 'It is well known that the Greeks, past masters of aesthetics, massaged to the point of "sculpturing" their body. The identical "sculpturing" has now been attained by modern science in the form of a powered apparatus – Aro-Lady.' Janine Harvey, an art student, user of such a vibratory bra claims: 'I love it. It's quite small, just like an ordinary bra except that it's made of spiral vibrators and has a battery in the cleavage. I wear it under a chunky Bohemian jersey. No one knows it's there – except my friend. But I walk through the streets in a sort of lovely erotic tizzy. Especially the super-market.'

A Battersea Health Inspector tells me: 'One of my jobs is to call in when someone dies without relatives to take control of his effects. Recently I was called in to an old man who had died in bed. When I visited the premises, which were squalid and rat-infested, I was surprised to see what seemed to be a second figure lying in the bed beside him. It was a life-sized dummy, made from stockings, a skirt, an old jumper, cardboard face taken from a cinema poster of Ava Gardner, a huge auburn wig. The model was stuffed with old rags and a bolster. It had stuffed handkerchiefs for breasts and a couple of marbles, held in by safety pins, for nipples. The Telly was still going . . .'

Notes

Holiday Camps:

Britain's Holiday Camps, unique institutions, virtually unknown abroad, are now used by one and a half million campers each year. About six per cent of all those who go on holiday. Holiday camps began in the thirties, but really multiplied after the last war. Not all are as big and brash as the one I describe here. (This is in fact a composite picture, based on various different holiday camps, each run by a different proprietor, with some characteristics taken from each.) Some have only a few hundred people each week. Many have five hundred to a thousand and others have many thousands of inmates.

Package Trip:

Five million British now holiday abroad every year. Large sections of the Med and other places are being tailored to fit them... They go mainly on package tours costing between about thirty and eighty pounds for a fortnight, including travel out there, accommodation and food, excluding drinks, excursions, and, of course, shopping.

Occasionally agencies which organize these package trips fold after taking the money, leaving tourists stranded in some foreign part foodless and bedless. More British foreign tourists (one million) go to Spain than to anywhere else and of these the highest density is in Palma, Majorca. The hotels here multiply by about ten per cent every year. Majorcans say that if it goes on much longer the island will surely sink.

Seaside:

Sixty per cent of the British now holiday away from home: Three quarters of them still go to the British seaside. The number is still slowly rising.

Some other books published by Penguins are described overleaf

THE PENGUIN PRIVATE EYE

Some Opinions of PRIVATE EYE

'These outrageous libels are not in the public interest' – Edward Martell

'I enjoy Private Eye more than I can say' – Baroness Asquith

'When are you going to develop a point of view?' – Kenneth Tynan

'Long may you flourish' – Anthony Wedgwood Benn

'God rot the lot of you' – Dr Jonathan Miller

A brand-new guide to the London scene . . .

LEN DEIGHTON'S LONDON DOSSIER

From the world-famous author of
Funeral in Berlin and *Billion Dollar Brain*
The brightest, best-informed, best-value guide to the new London,
its bars, bistros, boutiques, and byways; each chapter written by
a leading London journalist (the contributors include Nicholas
Tomalin, Drusilla Beyfus, Milton Shulman, Frank Norman and
others), the whole book edited and annotated by Len Deighton
with the zest and attention to detail that have made his spy-
thrillers world bestsellers. No visitor to Britain can afford to be
without this brand new, bang-up-to-date, hugely entertaining
vade-mecum.